ideals
THANKSGIVING

Thankfulness is an attribute,
A quality of life,
Which can make existence sweeter
And lighten every strife.
To appreciate is golden;
To say so is divine,
And thankfulness should come each day,
Not wait for special time.
Thanksgiving Day is every day;
November brings it near,
Remembering with grateful hearts
The blessings of all year.

　　　　　Mary A. Barnard

ISBN 0-8249-1006-0

IDEALS—Vol. 38, No. 7 October MCMLXXXI. IDEALS (ISSN 0019-137X) is published eight times a year, January, February, April, June, July, September, October, November by IDEALS PUBLISHING CORPORATION, 11315 Watertown Plank Road, Milwaukee, Wis. 53226 Second class postage paid at Milwaukee, Wisconsin. Copyright © MCMLXXXI by IDEALS PUBLISHING CORPORATION. Postmaster, please send form 3579 to Ideals Publishing Corporation, Post Office Box 2100, Milwaukee, Wis. 53201 All rights reserved. Title IDEALS registered U.S. Patent Office.
Published simultaneously in Canada.

ONE-YEAR SUBSCRIPTION—eight consecutive issues as published—$15.95
TWO-YEAR SUBSCRIPTION—sixteen consecutive issues as published—$27.95
SINGLE ISSUES—$3.50

The cover and entire contents of IDEALS are fully protected by copyright and must not be reproduced in any manner whatsoever. Printed and bound in U.S.A.

Publisher, James A. Kuse
Managing Editor, Ralph Luedtke
Editor/Ideals, Colleen Callahan Gonring
Associate Editor, Linda Robinson
Production Manager, Mark Brunner
Photographic Editor, Gerald Koser
Copy Editor, Barbara Nevid
Art Editor, Duane Weaver

An Autumn Blessing

Alice Leedy Mason

Bless us, Lord, the fall wind blows;
    The winter storms begin.
Bless this house in which we dwell
    And keep us snug within.
Bless the walls, the chimney top,
    Likewise the thumb-turned latch;
Bless the cat beside the hearth,
    The mouse he tries to catch.
Bless the books that line the shelves,
    The hands that gentle things,
That bake the loaves, make the beds,
    And bless the heart that sings.

Let laughter live within this house;
    Bless children as they play.
Bless all who knock upon the door
    And loved ones far away.
Bless the teapot steaming hot,
    The little cakes so fair.
Bless all who call this house a home
    With peace and love to share.
Bless harvest hoards in cellar bins,
    The rooftop firm and tall.
Give with these autumn blessings
    A thankful heart to all.

A Thanksgiving Meditation

Bernice Maddux

Traditionally we set aside a definite and special day of each year to pause and be thankful for all that we have received in the way of blessings in our lives. The rest of the year, I'm afraid, many of us take these same blessings for granted, shoving them thoughtlessly into the November-football-turkey-cranberry sauce-and-pumpkin pie slot, to dispose of them as a unit on Thanksgiving Day.

How we limit ourselves in the giving of thanks and the counting of blessings!

We know that enumeration of our gifts is as futile as counting the stars in the galaxy or the glistening sands along the seashore. Our finite minds are incapable; our time too short. But, even though completing the job is impossible, we should feel compelled to make a start.

Please accept this, our note of thanks, Dear God, for the liberality You have shown us, your children. We are grateful for the wonderful blessings of the past and present and the hopes we hold for the future.

Thank You for your omnipotence and boundless love, which carries us through tragedies and reverses and stands us firmly on our feet again for the uncertain journey ahead.

There is consolation in the knowledge that if there is a breakdown in communication, it is we who have pulled away, not You. And, for the forgiveness included in this package deal, we humbly thank You. We may err and err again; but, thanks to your living, forgiving spirit, when repentance is felt and properly expressed, there is yet hope for us.

If ever we are prone to question or doubt your love, dear Father, please cause us to look back at the cross and start again from there, letting You guide our stubborn and stumbling feet into the path You have charted for us.

We thank You for America and for the peace and security we feel here. Keep her always on her toes. Keep those by whom she is peopled busy with the task of driving hate, tyranny, greed, and oppression from her door.

We thank You for families. May they grow in unity and love and service to Thee. Let the words disintegration, generation gap, and out-of-date become obsolete descriptives where the family is concerned. We know that families are God-ordained. Help us to believe with all our hearts that they can and will be God-sustained.

Thank You for our children, those fragile bundles of clay which we strive with uncertain hands to mold into honorable men and women to carry on your work. Thank You for the look of trust in our babies' eyes, for our teens, who try our patience to the limit but reward us with love and appreciation when we least expect it, and for our married children, who can manage their homes perfectly without us but still ask our advice and still call our house "home."

We thank You for home, for the comfort and security and serenity it affords us, and for the spirit of love and helpfulness that abides there.

Though we are inexperienced at giving thanks for dark days, meager beginnings, failures, adversities, struggles, uncertainties, pain, sorrow, and weaknesses, make us realize, Father, that even in these there are hidden blessings and an unrecognizable balm for the soul in our dependence upon Thee.

Make us believe that dark days are just a prelude to brighter ones, a dreaded but quite necessary tunnel that will inevitably lead us into the sunshine again.

Help us to realize that from meager beginnings comes a greater and much fuller appreciation for any measure of success we might attain.

Show us how to use failures, struggles, and uncertainties as necessary stepping-stones to achieving worthwhile and desired goals in life.

Make us thankful for pain and sorrow in that it brings an appreciation and thankfulness for the absence of it, and causes us to sympathize, search out, and be helpful to others who are experiencing it.

Help us to look our weaknesses squarely in the face, in the knowledge that in overcoming them there is strength.

So what if we missed the brass ring? Show us that only through reaching can we attain full stature, and that not until we have sailed tempestuous seas can we experience fully the joys of a placid one.

Teach us that failure presents a series of lessons to be learned and give us open minds to learn them.

Impress upon us that sin has its inception only in a fertile heart. Help us to be about uprooting it in its infancy and planting in its stead good deeds and pure seeds of faith.

Keep us mindful to be thankful not only for the evident blessings of splendor and magnificence, but those blessings as well that we rarely recognize as such, those we must search for and often overlook.

Though we may never reach the end of the rainbow, make our hearts thankful that we are able to view it from any angle.

Let Thanksgiving know no season, no bounds, no limitations, and become a permanent fixture in our lives.

So many have given thanks for so little; let us never forget to give thanks for so much.

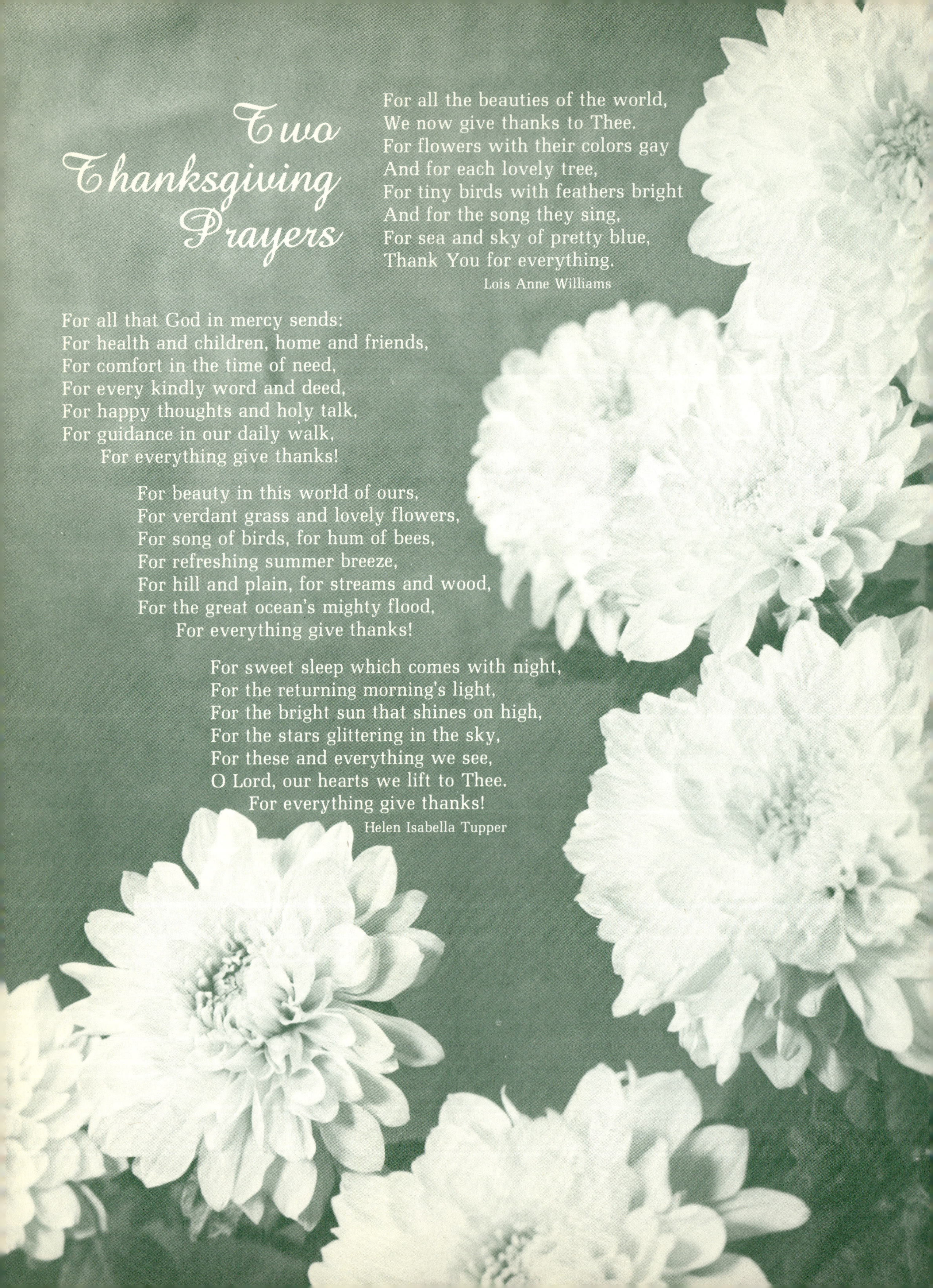

Two Thanksgiving Prayers

For all the beauties of the world,
We now give thanks to Thee.
For flowers with their colors gay
And for each lovely tree,
For tiny birds with feathers bright
And for the song they sing,
For sea and sky of pretty blue,
Thank You for everything.

                Lois Anne Williams

For all that God in mercy sends:
For health and children, home and friends,
For comfort in the time of need,
For every kindly word and deed,
For happy thoughts and holy talk,
For guidance in our daily walk,
    For everything give thanks!

    For beauty in this world of ours,
    For verdant grass and lovely flowers,
    For song of birds, for hum of bees,
    For refreshing summer breeze,
    For hill and plain, for streams and wood,
    For the great ocean's mighty flood,
        For everything give thanks!

        For sweet sleep which comes with night,
        For the returning morning's light,
        For the bright sun that shines on high,
        For the stars glittering in the sky,
        For these and everything we see,
        O Lord, our hearts we lift to Thee.
            For everything give thanks!

                Helen Isabella Tupper

Ideals' Best-Loved Poets

Edith Shaw Butler

Poetry written by Edith Shaw Butler has been frequently selected to appear in issues of Ideals over the last twenty years. A native and resident of Massachusetts, she developed a compelling, lifelong interest in roaming and observing the natural world of her surrounding countryside. Fortunately, she has been effective in translating this inspiration into words. Attending Massachusetts Teachers College, teaching school and marrying J. Kenneth Butler marked her early adult years. The Butler family grew to include two children and four grandchildren. Throughout forty-five years of active writing, her verses have been printed in more than forty publications such as *The Christian Science Monitor* and other religious periodicals. Her poems have been included in several anthologies and the poetry journals *The Lyric, Kaleidograph* and *Wings;* many have been set to music and published. She has been a regular contributor to *American Agriculturist* during much of her life. In the sharing of insights and fascinations within the lines of her poems, Edith Shaw Butler's company has been enriching to countless readers.

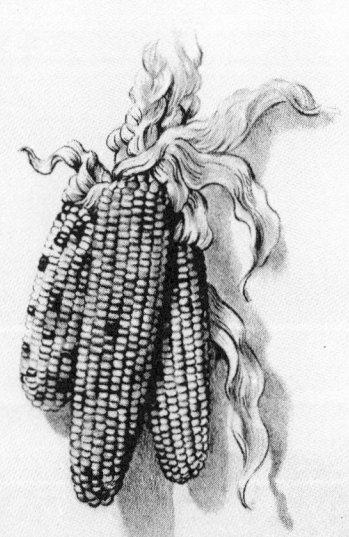

A Poem for Thanksgiving

Give thanks for simple things today:
A sturdy roof, our daily bread,
A kettle singing on the fire,
And seasoned wood piled in the shed.

Give thanks for beauty, crimson leaves
Against a sky of gentian blue,
For fruitfulness and harvestings,
For sudden song and laughter, too.

For health and strength to do our work,
For comradeship along the way,
For life, the greatest gift of all,
We keep in gratitude, this day.

Reasons for Thanksgiving

To have food enough and a place to dwell,
To have work to do and to do it well,

To find the comfort when things go wrong
In a bit of prayer or a snatch of song,

To know good books and share their worth,
To plant bright flowers in rich brown earth,

To have true friends—this is living
And reason enough for Thanksgiving.

Drifts o'er the Land

This is autumn wealth untold:

Maples flaming; bronze and gold
Elms against the clear blue sky;
An orchard where ripe apples lie
Half-hidden by the uncut grass;
Crimson sumac, sassafras,
And classic oaks that overlook
Smoky asters by the brook;
Orange bittersweet, corn in shocks;
In my garden, lingering phlox;

Harvests gathered, harvests stored—
Infinite blessings of the Lord.
Why should the heart hold any less
Than a deep abiding thankfulness?

After Harvestings

Corn in the crib and hay in the mow,
Scarce a red leaf on the bough;

Fruit in the bin, wood piled high,
Birch and maple seasoned dry;

Cattle home from the pasture again,
Sheep herded into their winter pen;

Cabbages heaped on the toolshed floor;
Let the snow come and the wild wind roar!

Now is the season the farmer holds dear,
Content with the gatherings of the year.

Countryman's Thanksgiving

Lord, I thank Thee for such things:
Autumn leaves and harvestings,
Fragrant hay in bulging mows,
Feathered flocks and leaf-brown cows,
Pumpkins on the big barn floor,
Cabbages—a hearty store,
Blessing of rain and sun,
Roof and fire when day is done,
Bending bough and laden vine,
Waving grain—all gifts of Thine;
For the things that I hold dear,
Keep me thankful all the year.

Freedom from Want

The good things of the earth are gathered now
To make the heart of man rejoice this day,
Remembering the gifts of field and bough,
The rich abundance he has stored away.
But though he plows the land and plants the seed,
It must have sun and rain to make it grow
To satisfy the age-old human need.
Grateful, he thinks from whom all blessings flow.
The stubble field marks where the land rests, sere
And brown, in quietness until the spring.
After the bright fulfillment of the year,
There comes this season of remembering;
And so he gathers loved ones in to share
His feast of harvesting with heartfelt prayer.

God Bless This Home

Bert Whitehouse

God bless this home in which we live;
God bless its every part.
God grant it peace and sweet content.
God grace our every heart.

God bless each portal of this home;
Let friendship light each way.
Let loving kindred fellowship
Be ours herein, we pray.

God bless each soul that enters in
And bless him on his way.
God enter in this home of ours
And bless it every day.

My ABC's of Fruits and Vegetables

Caroline M. Nye

Some folks are crazy about meat and fish;
I like them, but they're not my favorite dish.
Fresh fruits and vegetables, they are for me—
Fresh fruits and vegetables, from A to Z.

A is for asparagus and artichoke hearts,
and big juicy apples and apricot tarts.

B is for blueberries, beans and red beets,
and golden bananas—my favorite treats.

C is for carrots and celery for crunching,
and corn on the cob for mighty good munching.

D is for dates—eat them stuffed, or just plain,
in a fruitcake at Christmas, or out in the rain.

E is for eggplant you bake in a sauce,
and endive looks pretty in salads you toss.

F is for fig bars—I like them—I do!
and also fruit cocktail, my favorite too.

G is for green peppers and grapefruit and grits,
and all kinds of grapes, but don't swallow the pits!

H is for huckleberries, good in a pie,
and honeydew melons; just give them a try.

I is for Italian plums, good for snacking,
a wonderful fruit when you're picnic-lunch packing.

J is for jam—different kinds for your toast;
peach jam and grape are the ones I like most.

K is for Kosher dill pickles—they're great,
and kale and kohlrabi are also first-rate.

L is for lima beans, lettuce and limes,
and cold lemonade, so refreshing sometimes.

M is for mangoes, delicious to eat,
and muskmelon slices—they're always a treat.

N is for nectarines, smiling at me;
I think they come from a happiness tree.

O is for onions to give foods more flavor,
and olives and oranges to taste and to savor.

P is for pineapples, peaches and pears,
and potatoes to bake when we're hungry as bears.

Q is for quince, used for jelly or jam,
and spiced quince preserves, which I like with ham.

R is for raspberries, rhubarb and rice,
and relish for hot dogs, and raisins are nice.

S is for spinach and squash that you bake,
and red, ripe strawberries for making shortcake.

T is for tomatoes—I'd eat them all day,
fresh sliced, in a salad, or most any way.

U is unhappy; he doesn't have one,
not one fruit or vegetable under the sun.

V is for vegetable soup—what a joy,
with alphabet letters for each girl and boy.

W is for watermelon—such a delight;
I think I could eat it from morning till night.

X was forgotten when foods got a name;
no fruit or vegetable can poor "X" claim.

Y is for yogurt just chock-full of cherries,
fresh golden peaches, or succulent berries.

Z is for zucchini, and it's sure to please,
served hot with butter, tomatoes and cheese.

Thanksgiving

Thanksgiving is crowning the autumn
　With gold from the maple leaves
And draping around her fair shoulders
　A scarf that the woodbine weaves.

　It's giving her raiment of orange,
　　So bright with the pumpkin's glow,
　And weaving her sandals of russet
　　That only fall grasses know.

　　It's crowning our labor with blessings,
　　　More precious than autumn's gold.
　　It's bringing us family reunions
　　　With all of the joy they hold.

　　　It's filling each storehouse with treasures
　　　　From harvests abundant and fine
　　　That we may have plenty for sharing
　　　　With all at Thanksgiving time.

　　　　　　　Josephine Millard

In Defense of an Old Wall

The old wall wears the autumn well.
It knows the creeper, red and gold,
The burnished green of moss, the twine
Of ivy with its gripping hold.

It neighbors with the thistle bloom,
The aster in her roadside beauty;
Long years ago, when it was new,
It must have had some sort of duty.

But now it sits content and wears
Its sumac-studded shawl.
Its useful days are gone, you say?

Perhaps you do not know that all
The strength of our traditions dwells
In old things that have served us well.

Helen Baker Adams

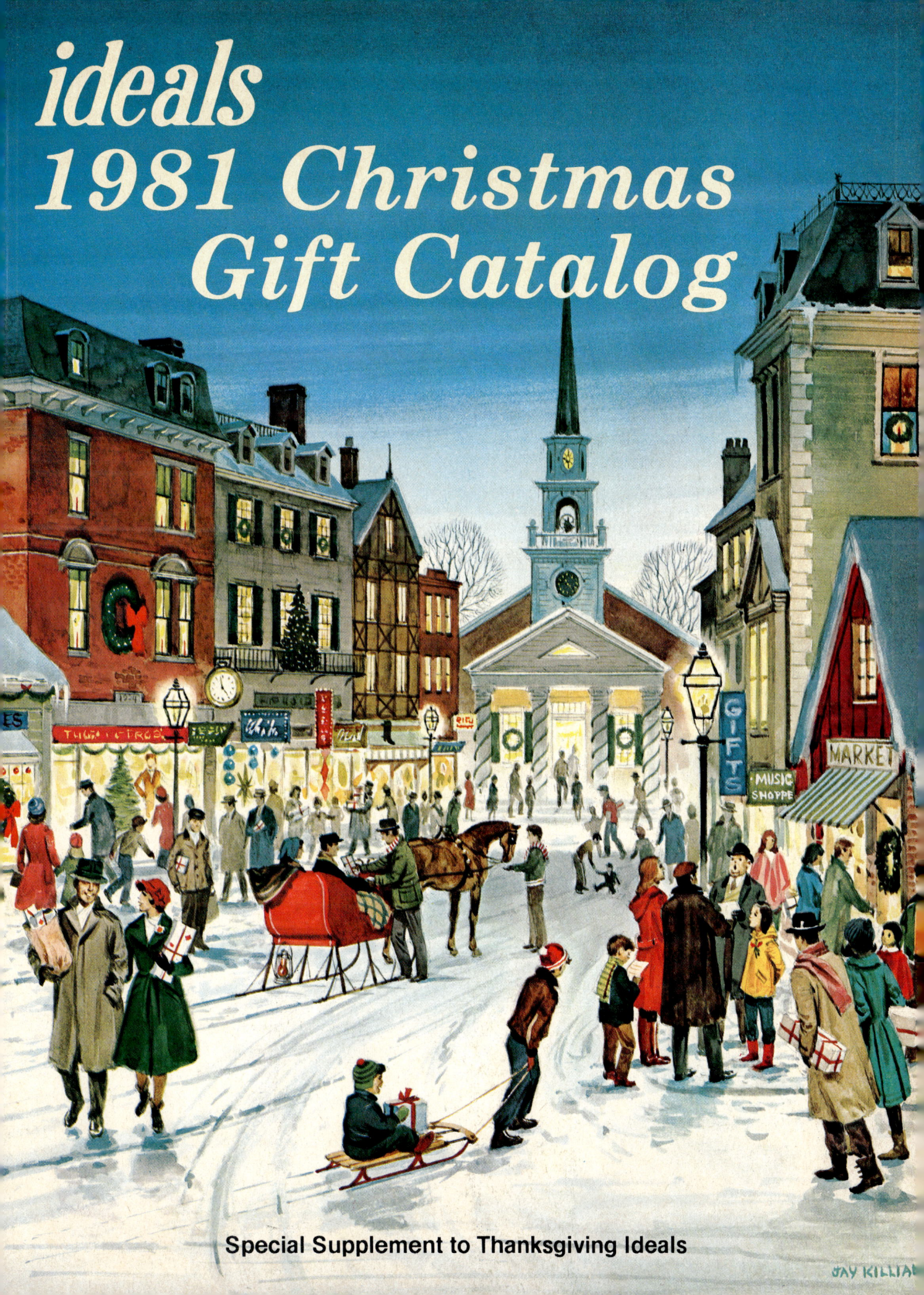

Season's Greetings!

Dear Ideals' Friend,

We at Ideals want to take this opportunity to wish you and your family a blessed and joyful holiday season.

We are pleased to offer you this 1981 Christmas catalog . . . bigger, better and more diverse than in years past. As you page through this catalog, you will find that Ideals has expanded its publishing efforts. This is most evident in the sections devoted to cookbooks, children's books and the new Successful Home Improvement series.

We've also included an announcement of the Country Kitchen Cookbook Plan. We invite you to participate in this rather unique approach to expanding your cookbook library.

We hope you'll find many gift ideas and books that you and your family can personally enjoy within these pages. Many of our beautiful editions are offered at special budget-saving prices!

We are offering you a special bonus . . . on orders of $20.00 or more, you have a choice of free gifts! You may include subscriptions and catalog items to qualify for the bonus! Sorry, but the Country Kitchen Plan cannot be included.

To order, use the order form found in the center of this catalog or pick up the phone and call us TOLL FREE 1-800-558-4343. To ensure holiday delivery, we ask that you place your order before December 1.

We value you as a customer and as a friend. It is a pleasure to serve you. We hope that your Holiday season is one that gives you pleace and joy and that the New Year brings you good fortune and happiness.

Sincerely,

Donald A. Gottschalk

Donald A. Gottschalk
Chief Executive Officer

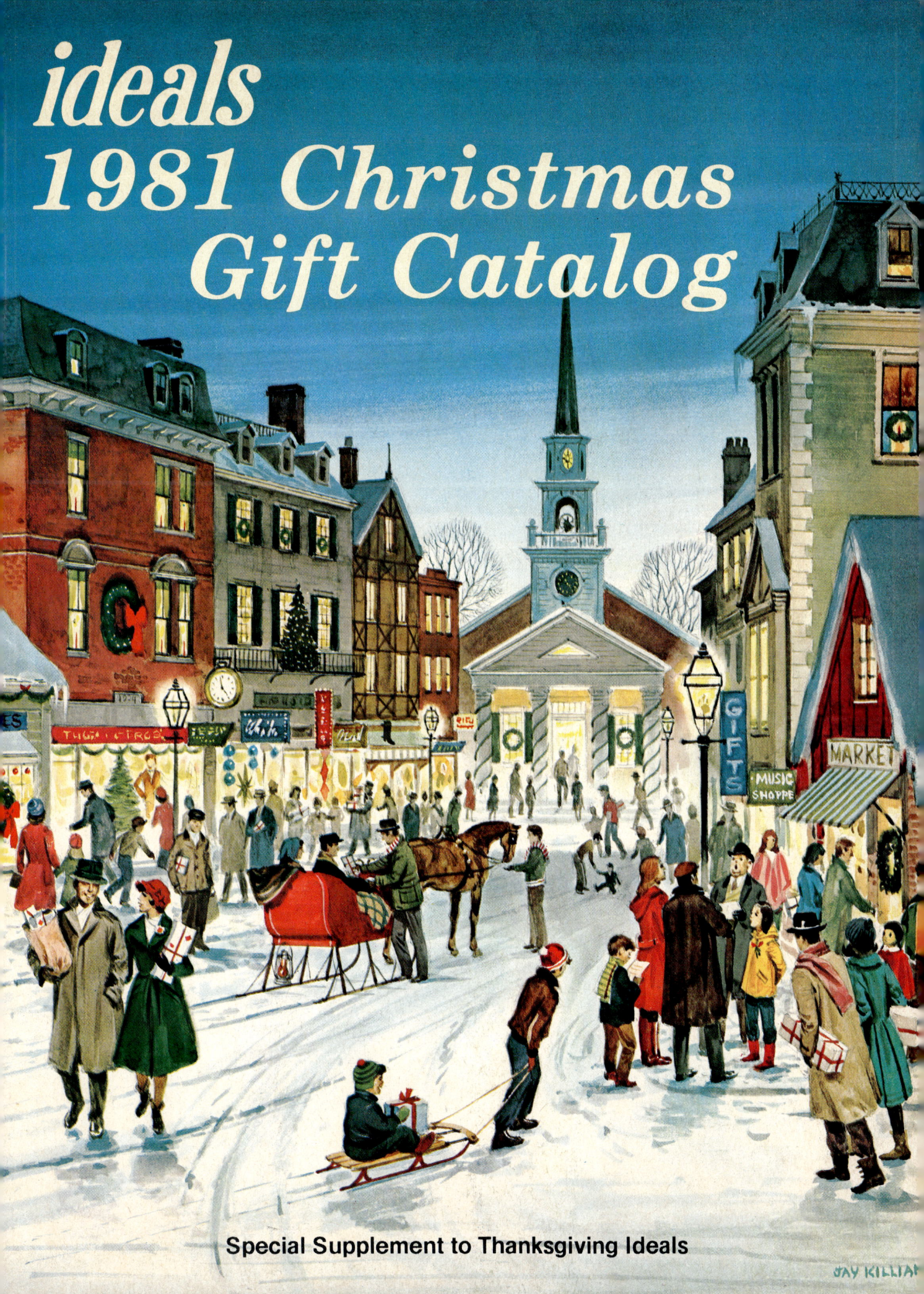

Season's Greetings!

Dear Ideals' Friend,

We at Ideals want to take this opportunity to wish you and your family a blessed and joyful holiday season.

We are pleased to offer you this 1981 Christmas catalog . . . bigger, better and more diverse than in years past. As you page through this catalog, you will find that Ideals has expanded its publishing efforts. This is most evident in the sections devoted to cookbooks, children's books and the new Successful Home Improvement series.

We've also included an announcement of the Country Kitchen Cookbook Plan. We invite you to participate in this rather unique approach to expanding your cookbook library.

We hope you'll find many gift ideas and books that you and your family can personally enjoy within these pages. Many of our beautiful editions are offered at special budget-saving prices!

We are offering you a special bonus . . . on orders of $20.00 or more, you have a choice of free gifts! You may include subscriptions and catalog items to qualify for the bonus! Sorry, but the Country Kitchen Plan cannot be included.

To order, use the order form found in the center of this catalog or pick up the phone and call us TOLL FREE 1-800-558-4343. To ensure holiday delivery, we ask that you place your order before December 1.

We value you as a customer and as a friend. It is a pleasure to serve you. We hope that your Holiday season is one that gives you pleace and joy and that the New Year brings you good fortune and happiness.

Sincerely,

Donald A. Gottschalk

Donald A. Gottschalk
Chief Executive Officer

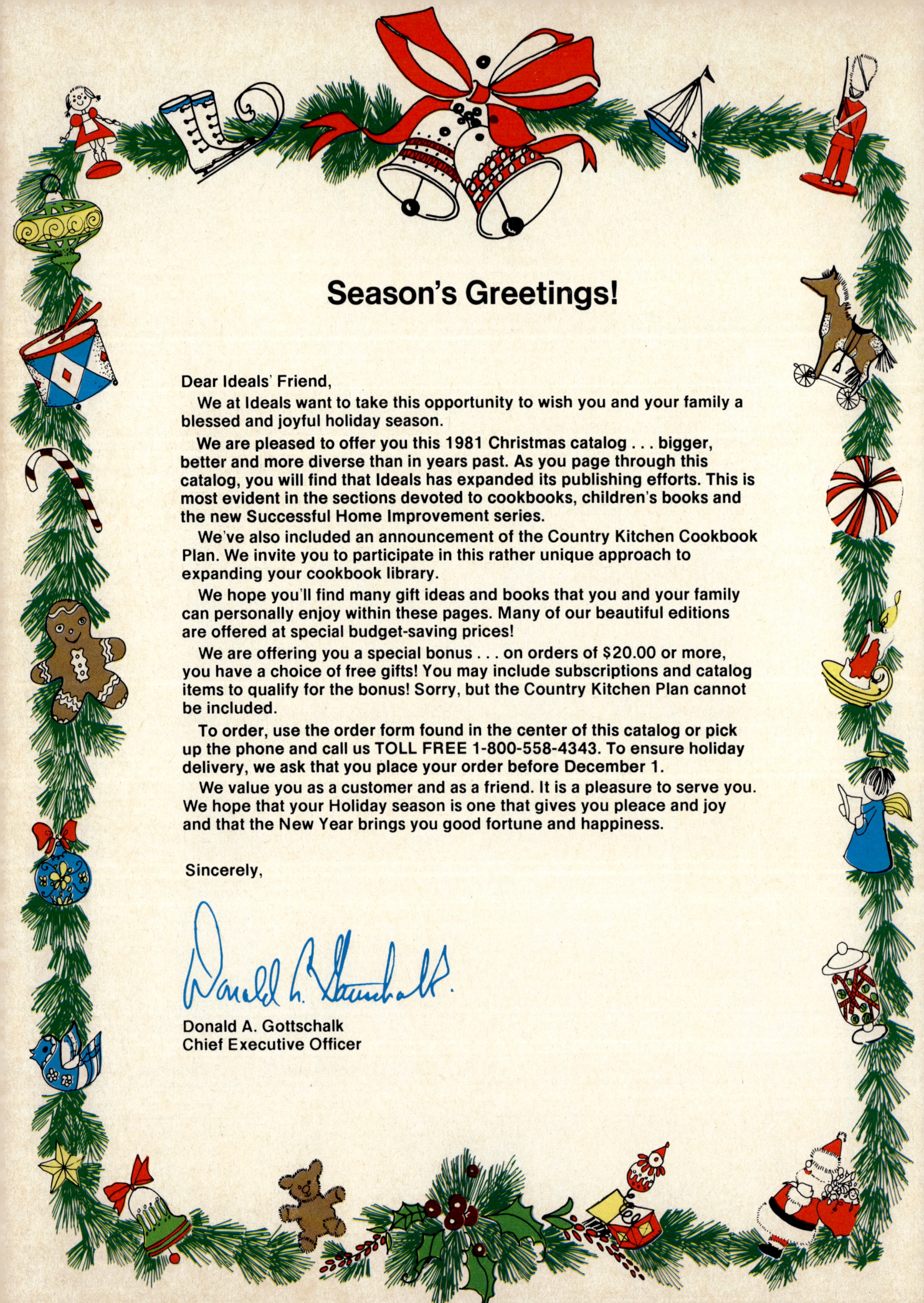

Christmas Ideals

CHRISTMAS IDEALS has been a treasured part of family holidays for almost forty years. Heart-warming prose and poetry portray the many blessings the yuletide season brings. Rich color photographs and original art lavishly illustrate favorite stories that both the young and the young-at-heart look forward to each year. The new 1981 Christmas Ideals highlights: the magnificent attributes of winter in "Northwoods Notebook"; a charming tale, "Santa Making His List", accompanied by a Norman Rockwell painting; and the Nativity Story, depicted in biblical verse and old master paintings. Truly, this is a keepsake issue! What better way to express your sentiments this season than with a gift of Christmas Ideals?
80 pages   1-007 $3.50

Special ... 5 copies   7-984 $12.95

 **C H R I**

LET'S CELEBRATE CHRISTMAS is a delightful volume featuring traditions and special holiday celebrations from all over the U.S.A. Perhaps New Mexico's "luminarias" could brighten your family's gathering this year. Or, Christmas customs in Old Sturbridge, Massachusetts might appeal to you. Whatever your choice, this book is sure to become a favorite at Christmas.
80 pages   4-289 $3.95

DECORATING FOR THE HOLIDAYS is indispensible for anyone who wants to create a festive look for their home this season. Expert advice features ideas for advent through twelfth night including wreaths, table pieces and fresh and permanent arrangements. Step-by-step instructions along with color photos of the finished products are included. Make lovely arrangements to keep or to give as gifts.
64 pages   4-286 $2.95

CHRISTMAS AROUND THE WORLD is a colorful collection of unique celebrations and Christmas customs from twenty countries. Featured are France, Germany, England, Poland and Italy to name but a few. For your reading enjoyment or to add a festive flair to family celebrations.
64 pages   4-009 $3.95

FAVORITE CHRISTMAS CAROLS features a popular collection of traditional carols accompanied with delightful artwork. Perfect for carrolling groups this season!
32 pages   8-474 $1.50

THE CHRISTMAS MIRACLE is a heart-warming account of the first Christmas as witnessed by the people at the manger. Interwoven into this narrative are special poems and prose on the true meaning of Christmas. Old master paintings and beautiful contemporary art accompanies the text.
80 pages   2-046 $3.95

A TIME FOR GIVING discusses the true meaning of this important holiday: how God gave the greatest gift to mankind and how we can incorporate His gift into our own lives at Christmas and all year long. By noted author and lecturer, Jill Briscoe, this volume would be a welcome addition to any home.
80 pages   2-069 $5.95

Keep the spirit of Christmas . . . the joy and peace . . . all year 'round with *ideals*

Celebrate the seasons and our major holidays with 8 beautiful NEW ISSUES each year

- **RENEWALS**
- **GIFTS**
- **SUBSCRIPTIONS**

Save up to 50%

EACH NEW ISSUE FEATURES:
- 80 advertising-free pages of exquisite quality.
- Full-color photographs of nature, people, homes, interiors, crafts and antiques.
- Prose and photography combined to present informative articles.
- Poetry and fascinating short stories.
- Art reproductions to frame.

Renewals – send your renewal with your catalog order and get a free gift (combined order of $20.00 or more).

Gifts – remember the special people in your life with an uplifting gift subscription.

Subscriptions – give a gift of beauty to yourself and to your family.

Save 43% • 8 issues (1 year)
a $28.00 value — Only $15.95

Save 50% • 16 issues (2 years)
a $56.00 value — Only $27.95

Foreign & Canadian subscriptions add $4.00 per year for postage.

use the attached order form for your personal and gift subscriptions.

Christmas Treasury

CHRISTMAS TREASURY is a glorious portrayal of Christmas with Ideals. Our favorite stories, poems and illustrations are colorfully combined in this deluxe volume. One hundred and sixty pages will bring all of the wonder and magic of Christmas to you and to the special people in your lives. An outstanding value! Hardcover.
160 pages   4-006 $12.95

Special . . . 3 copies   7-974 $22.95

S·T·M·A·S

SEASON'S GREETINGS is a splendid collection of Christmas verse and photography. It's a colorful way of expressing your thoughts to family and friends this season and it will be treasured always for little more than the cost of a greeting card.
32 pages   4-029 $2.25

CHRISTMAS KITCHEN COOKBOOK contains delicious recipes to make holidays fun and festive! A tempting array of cookies, candies, relishes, jellies and snacks are but a few of the great taste ideas waiting for you!
64 pages   3-635 $2.95

MERRY CHRISTMAS vividly portrays the splendor of this holiday season with prose, poetry and colorful photography. A perfect way to say a special "I'm thinking of you" to friends and relatives!
32 pages   4-459 $2.25

GOURMET CHRISTMAS COOKBOOK offers over 200 delicious recipes for family celebrations and entertaining from appetizers and beverages to quick breads and desserts. The busy cook/hostess will be able to prepare tempting fare with a minimal amount of time and ingredients.
64 pages   3-613 $2.95

CHRISTMAS COOKBOOK features an outstanding collection of traditional holiday menu and gift ideas. These are our readers' favorite recipes, tested by generations. Give your family a special Christmas treat this year and prepare festive holiday fare from this superb volume!
64 pages   3-602 $2.95

CHRISTMAS AROUND THE WORLD COOKBOOK is a selection of menus for festive holiday dining from twenty countries. Choose a complete menu or select courses from different countries to give your Christmas celebration a foreign flair!
64 pages   3-008 $2.95

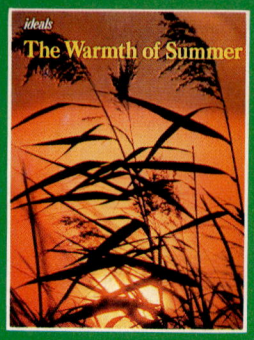
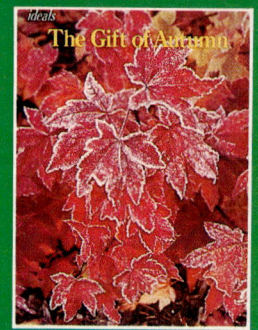

Four Seasons Gift Set

Celebrate the four seasons with Ideals! This set of four books, THE BEAUTY OF WINTER, THE JOY OF SPRING, THE WARMTH OF SUMMER and THE GIFT OF AUTUMN, beautifully details the special attributes of each season. Join well-known nature writers such as John Burroughs, Walt Whitman, Ralph Waldo Emerson and Henry David Thoreau. Outstanding color photography accompanies the text. A lasting gift to be enjoyed throughout the year.

THE BEAUTY OF WINTER	80 pages	4-073	$4.95
THE JOY OF SPRING	80 pages	4-063	$4.95
THE WARMTH OF SUMMER	80 pages	4-065	$4.95
THE GIFT OF AUTUMN	80 pages	4-072	$4.95
Special... Four Seasons Set		7-980	$15.50

G ❄ I ❄ F ❄ T

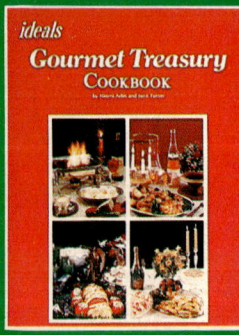

GOURMET TREASURY COOKBOOK is a superb volume containing over 700 delicious recipes for the busy cook and hostess. You'll find dozens of easy, taste-tempting suggestions for appetizers, soups, main dishes, vegetables, quick breads and desserts. Perfect for family meals, entertaining and holiday get-togethers. This is a gift you can be sure will be used again and again! Hardcover.
224 pages   3-024 $9.95

DOWN TO EARTH HOUSEPLANTS is a complete guide to plant care from purchasing healthy plants to decorating ideas. Color photographs and comprehensive descriptions of popular varieties are featured along with charts detailing light conditions, soil and water requirements and transplanting and propagation instructions. A handy reference volume for personal use or as a thoughtful gift.
68 pages   4-387 $2.95

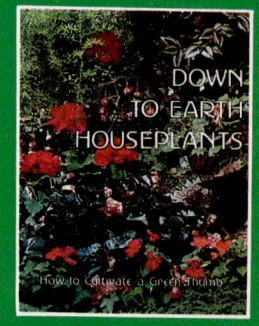

COUNTRY SCENE DIGEST presents the best of country living in this colorful edition. Enjoy recipes featuring down-home goodness, expert gardening tips and new craft ideas complete with step-by-step instructions plus much more! An outstanding value as a gift or for yourself!
224 pages   4-353 $6.95

THE IDEAL LIFE: 50 AND OVER is a comprehensive guide for those who wish to start pre-planning and enjoying the retirement years. Topics covered include: financial planning, ways to maintain physical and mental health, Medicare, Medicaid and Social Security and second careers.
224 pages   4-081 $5.95

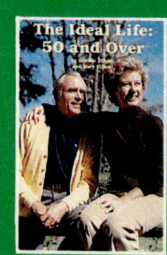

THE BEST OF WEIGHT WATCHERS MAGAZINE features a wealth of information for people who are weight-conscious. Highlights include delicious, low-calorie recipes, step-by-step exercises, fashion and make-up tips, how to keep your spirits up while losing weight and leisure time activities to aid in weight loss.
128 pages   4-621 $4.95

FLOWERS OF FRIENDSHIP is a lovely volume featuring the exquisite paintings of noted artist, Maryrose Wampler. Beautiful color plates capture the essence of wildflowers in their natural woodland settings. Touching poetry reflecting on the meaning of friendship is interwoven with the illustrations. A perfect gift to share with a friend!
80 pages   4-261 $3.95

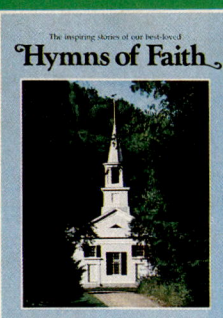
HYMNS OF FAITH contains favorite hymns and the story behind their creation. While most of these hymns have been beloved for generations, they will become even more special when you learn how they came into being.
80 pages   2-066 $3.95

QUIET REFLECTIONS AND TRANQUIL MOMENTS is a keepsake volume devoted to the poetry of Patience Strong, a favorite of our readers. The selections were personally chosen by the author and an outstanding collection of color photographs illustrate the peace and tranquility found in her writings.
80 pages   4-067 $3.95

LOOK TO THIS DAY is an inspiring book of verse based on the Sanskrit. The thoughtfully selected poems will be read again and again. Beautiful color photographs complement the text.
80 pages   2-052 $3.95

A TIME FOR LIVING discusses the new life Christ offered to mankind through his death and resurrection. Noted author, Jill Briscoe, shows us how we can live this new life to our fullest ability in the Christian community.
80 pages   2-078 $5.95

S✻H✻O✻P

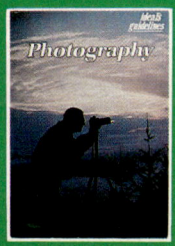
PHOTOGRAPHY will give you expert advice on how to make your pictures turn out professionally. Whether you're a beginner or an advanced photographer, this pocket companion will be indispensible!
96 pages   4-900 $2.95

VEGETABLE GARDENING GUIDE illustrates the ABC's of vegetable gardening for those who wish to enjoy the flavor of home-grown foods. Planning, types of seeds and sources, soil conditions, problems and pests and harvesting are but a few of the topics discussed. Plan now for next spring's garden!
96 pages   4-000 $2.95

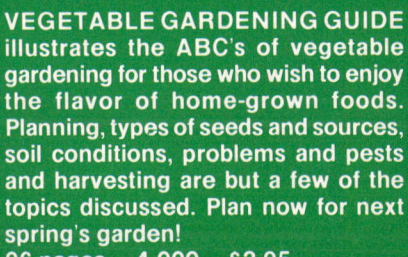

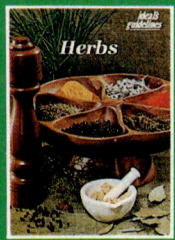
HERBS is a handy reference featuring everything you wanted to know about growing and using herbs. Various types of gardens, medicinal and culinary uses and methods of preserving herbs are discussed.
96 pages   4-903 $2.95

HOUSEHOLD ENERGY SAVING GUIDE tells today's homeowners how to trim energy costs with a minimum investment of time and money. Insulation, types of heat and greenhouses are just a few of the topics featured to help make your home energy efficient.
96 pages   4-010 $2.95

PRESERVING FOOD is a complete guide to preserving fruits and vegetables. Various methods of preserving foods are discussed as well as the necessary preparation, equipment and storage conditions. Enjoy the satisfaction and delicious taste of preserving food!
96 pages   4-905 $2.95

FAMILY FIRST AID GUIDE gives information everyone should know about emergency first aid treatment. Safety measures you can take around the home to prevent accidents and basic first aid supplies as well as specific types of injuries and their immediate care are discussed.
96 pages   4-011 $2.95
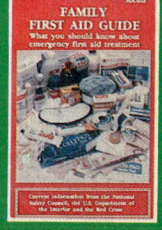

Special . . . all six guidelines for only $13.50!
a $17.70 value!   7-985 $13.50

CHRISTMAS GREETINGS will say so much more than just a greeting card! Let this delightful booklet express your holiday sentiments for you! A fine selection of seasonal verse is accompanied by brilliant color photography. Receive extra savings when you purchase sets of twelve! Complete with envelopes.
5-819 $1.00
Special... set of 12   7-977 $9.95

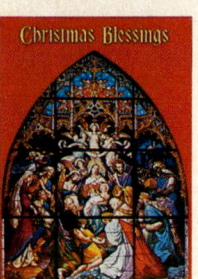

CHRISTMAS BLESSINGS will convey the special meaning of the most important Christian holiday in joyous verse. Beautiful photography complements biblical passages and heartfelt poetry. Special savings are offered on sets of twelve! Complete with envelopes.
5-820 $1.00
Special... set of 12   7-978 $9.95

Special set of 6 Greetings
and 6 Blessings   7-979 $9.95

SATISFACTION GUARANTEE

If, after receiving your order, you find your books are not as beautiful and inspiring as you expected, just return them to us in the original wrapper marked "return to sender." We will cancel the invoice or refund your money.

IF ORDER FORM IS MISSING...
Order by title, code and price.
Send to:
Ideals Publishing Corp.
P.O. Box 2100
Milwaukee, WI 53201

GREETINGS

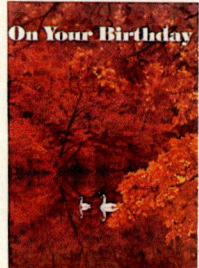 

All Occasion Booklets

This selection of all occasion greeting booklets will serve every need you have for greeting cards and yet say so much more! Each one has a special theme, beautifully expressed in thoughtful verse and brilliant color photography and will be a lasting remembrance for the special people in your life! As a set, these twelve greeting booklets are an outstanding value! Complete with envelopes.

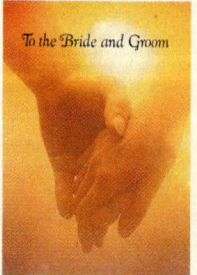 

TO COMFORT YOU	5-826	$1.00
A SPECIAL THANK YOU	5-812	$1.00
FROM THIS DAY FORWARD	5-774	$1.00
GOD'S ORCHARD	5-806	$1.00
WITH SYMPATHY	5-807	$1.00
GET WELL SOON	5-816	$1.00
ON YOUR BIRTHDAY	5-815	$1.00
REMEMBERING YOUR ANNIVERSARY	5-779	$1.00
TO THE BRIDE AND GROOM	5-809	$1.00
YOU ARE MY FRIEND	5-777	$1.00
HAPPY BIRTHDAY	5-808	$1.00
TO THE HAPPY PARENTS	5-772	$1.00
Special... set of all 12	7-973	$9.95

IDEALS' BINDER
BEAUTIFUL BINDER HOLDS 8 ISSUES OF IDEALS!

An Ideals' binder is a must for anyone who treasures the lasting beauty of Ideals. Our colorful cover design features the four seasons captured in brilliant photography on a deluxe vinyl exterior. Metal rod binding eliminates any unsightly hole punching. Sturdy construction protects your issues and prevents damage. Perfect for your own collection or as a gift to the special person you give an Ideals subscription to.
10-713 $5.95

IDEALS' COOKBOOK VIEWER
CONVENIENT LUCITE VIEWER PROTECTS BOOKS!

Our handy cookbook viewer is made of strong, durable lucite. It gives you a clear view of the cookbook page you are using while holding the book firmly in place. Smudges and spatters wipe clean. The viewer folds flat for storage. It may also be used for the home repairman, craftsman or student. A unique gift to be used year round.
10-716 $6.95

How To Order . . .

BY MAIL

1. Enter your complete name and address (including zip code) in the area provided in the upper left hand corner of the order blank.
2. Enter QUANTITY to be ordered for each item in the appropriate column under quantity.

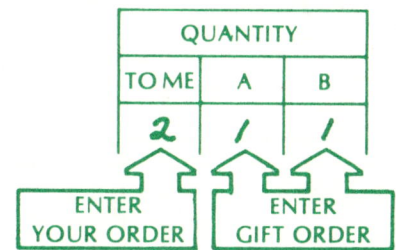

For your personal order enter quantity in column "To Me." All items entered in columns "A" or "B" will be sent as gifts from you to the persons indicated in the corresponding gift address areas.

3. Enter AMOUNT (quantity x price) in the box provided for each item.
4. Total your complete catalogue order (including gift shipments) and enter in SUB TOTAL.
5. Add SUB TOTAL and POSTAGE and enter in TOTAL. Add tax if applicable.
6. Add SUBSCRIPTIONS enrolled on the special card in the catalog. If your GRAND TOTAL is $20.00 or more you may choose a FREE GIFT! See other side for details.

7. For your catalogue purchase indicate your choice of payment plans. If you are using your credit card, be sure to include your signature, expiration date and your complete account number. Separate the order form from the envelope, fold your order form, enclose your check or money order and your subscription card in the envelope and mail.

BY TELEPHONE

CALL TOLL FREE
1-800-558-4343

**Wisconsin Residents
Call Collect (414) 771-2700**

Ideals will be pleased to take your order by phone. Our telephone department is open Monday thru Friday, 8 AM to 4:30 PM (C.S.T.). For questions or product information, please call our regular office number, (414) 771-2774.

Thank you.

ideals PUBLISHING CORPORATION
P.O. BOX 2100
MILWAUKEE, WI 53201

B101

MY ADDRESS

YOUR NAME _____
ADDRESS _____
CITY _____
STATE _____ ZIP _____
TELEPHONE NO. _____

Remit in U.S. Currency
☐ Payment Enclosed
☐ Bill Me
☐ Charge my Master Charge
☐ Charge my BankAmericard/VISA   Exp. Date

Acct. No. ☐☐☐☐☐☐☐☐☐☐☐☐☐☐☐☐ ☐☐☐☐
SIGNATURE _____

FOR GIFT ORDERS:
- Fill in above section
- Fill in quantity A on order blank for 1st Gift Address; and quantity B for 2nd Gift Address.
- If additional gifts are to be ordered, write instructions on a plain sheet and enclose with your order.

GIFT ADDRESS A

Please send the items I have indicated to be shipped to ADDRESS A as gifts from me to my friend listed below:

GIFT NAME _____
ADDRESS _____
CITY _____
STATE _____ ZIP _____

GIFT ADDRESS B

Please send the items I have indicated to be shipped to ADDRESS B as gifts from me to my friend listed below:

GIFT NAME _____
ADDRESS _____
CITY _____
STATE _____ ZIP _____

ORDERING INSTRUCTIONS

QUANTITY
TO ME	A	B
2	1	1
↑ ENTER YOUR ORDER   ↑ ENTER GIFT ORDER

- Enter quantity to be ordered
- Enter your order
- Enter gift orders
- Enter amount (quantity x price) in box provided for each item.
- Total your order as indicated.
- To expedite your order, use our Toll Free Service 1-800-558-4343 WI. Residents Call Collect (414) 771-2700

CODE	TITLE	QUANTITY ME	A	B	PRICE	AMOUNT
	CHRISTMAS					
7-984	Special — 5 Christmas Ideals A $17.50 Value				$12.95 per 5	
1-007	1981 Christmas Ideals				$3.50	
4-289	Let's Celebrate Christmas				$3.95	
4-009	Christmas Around The World				$3.95	
2-046	The Christmas Miracle				$3.95	
4-286	Decorating For The Holidays				$2.95	
8-474	Favorite Christmas Carols				$1.50	
2-069	A Time For Giving				$5.95	
7-974	Special — 3 Christmas Treasury — A $38.85 Value				$22.95 per 3	
4-006	Christmas Treasury				$12.95	
4-029	Season's Greetings				$2.25	
4-459	Merry Christmas				$2.25	
3-602	Christmas Cookbook				$2.95	
3-635	Christmas Kitchen Ck Bk				$2.95	
3-613	Gourmet Christmas Ck Bk				$2.95	
3-008	Christmas Around World Ck Bk				$2.95	
	GIFT SHOP					
7-980	Special — 4 Seasons Set A $19.80 Value				$15.50 per set	
4-073	The Beauty of Winter				$4.95	
4-063	The Joy of Spring				$4.95	
4-065	The Warmth of Summer				$4.95	
4-072	The Gift of Autumn				$4.95	
3-024	Gourmet Treasury Ck Bk				$9.95	
4-353	Country Scene Digest				$6.95	
4-621	Best of Weight Watchers				$4.95	
4-387	Down To Earth Houseplants				$2.95	
4-081	Ideal Life: 50 And Over				$5.95	
4-261	Flowers of Friendship				$3.95	
2-066	Hymns of Faith				$3.95	
2-052	Look To This Day				$3.95	
4-067	Quiet Reflections/Moments				$3.95	
2-078	A Time For Living				$5.95	
7-985	Special — All 6 Guidelines A $17.70 Value				$13.50 per set	
4-900	Photography				$2.95	
4-903	Herbs				$2.95	
4-905	Preserving Foods				$2.95	
4-000	Vegetable Gardening				$2.95	
4-010	Household Energy Saving				$2.95	
4-011	Family First Aid				$2.95	
	GREETINGS					
7-977	Special — 12 Christmas Greetings — A $12.00 Value				$9.95 per set	
5-819	Christmas Greetings				$1.00	
7-978	Special — 12 Christmas Blessings — A $12.00 Value				$9.95 per 12	
5-820	Christmas Blessings				$1.00	
7-979	Special — 12 Pack — 6 Each Christmas & Blessings				$9.95 per 12	
7-973	Special — Variety Pack 1 Each of 12 Titles				$9.95 per pk.	
5-826	To Comfort You				$1.00	
5-812	A Special Thank You				$1.00	
5-774	From This Day Forward				$1.00	
5-806	God's Orchard				$1.00	
5-807	With Sympathy				$1.00	
5-816	Get Well Soon				$1.00	
5-815	On Your Birthday				$1.00	
5-779	Remembering/Anniversary				$1.00	
5-809	To The Bride And Groom				$1.00	
5-777	You Are My Friend				$1.00	
5-808	Happy Birthday				$1.00	
5-772	To The Happy Parents				$1.00	
	CHILDREN					
7-967	Offer A — 6 Good Friends A $5.70 Value				$4.95 per 6	
7-964	Offer B — 6 Good Friends A $5.70 Value				$4.95 per 6	
7-986	Special—5 Book Set—1 Each Titles Listed—A $13.40 Value				$10.95 per 5	
8-262	Dickens' Christmas Carol				$2.95	
8-498	The Night Before Christmas				$2.50	
8-454	The Story of Christmas				$2.50	
8-514	Amanda's Tree				$2.95	
8-448	Jolly Old Santa Claus				$2.50	

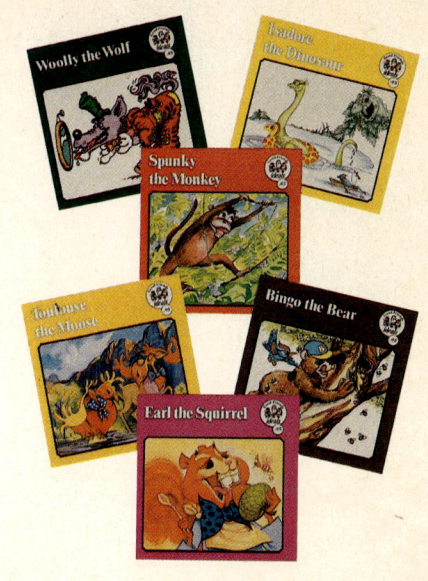

Perfect for Stocking Stuffers!

These spectacular, full-color 95¢ story books feature lovable animal characters in delightful adventure stories. Children will find some good lessons in life with Ideals' "Good Friends"! Perfect for stocking stuffers!

Offer A . . . a $5.70 value!
6 books   7-967 $4.95

Offer B . . . a $5.70 value!
6 books   7-964 $4.95

Offer A   Offer B

CHILDREN

Special . . . a $13.40 value!
5 book set   7-986 $10.95

DICKENS' CHRISTMAS CAROL
THE NIGHT BEFORE CHRISTMAS
STORY OF CHRISTMAS FOR CHILDREN
AMANDA'S TREE
JOLLY OLD SANTA CLAUS

THE STORY OF CHRISTMAS FOR CHILDREN tells the Nativity story in rhyming verse. Children can easily understand the special meaning of this important holiday. Beautiful artwork accompanies the text.
32 pages   8-454 $2.50

DICKENS' CHRISTMAS CAROL tells the ageless story of the true meaning of Christmas giving. Tiny Tim, Scrooge and the ghosts of Christmas come alive in beautiful color artwork. Make this story a holiday tradition for someone you love!
48 pages   8-262 $2.95

AMANDA'S TREE is a story of love and giving at Christmas time. A small girl shares a very special Christmas tree with those in need of cheer and finds that perhaps sharing is the best Christmas gift of all!
32 pages   8-514 $2.95

THE NIGHT BEFORE CHRISTMAS portrays Clement Moore's famous poem in beautiful full-color illustrations. Adults and children will both enjoy this delightful holiday tale!
32 pages   8-498 $2.50

JOLLY OLD SANTA CLAUS tells of the joyous activity at the North Pole as Santa and his elves prepare for the busiest night of the year . . . Christmas Eve! George Hinke's superb artwork complements the story.
32 pages   8-448 $2.50

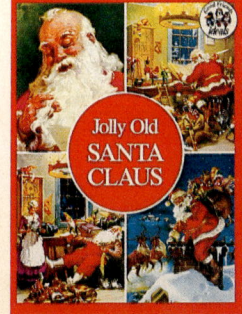

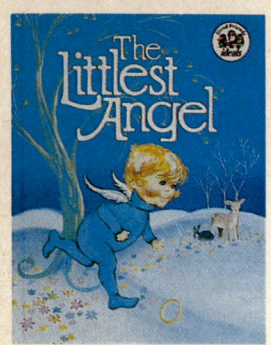
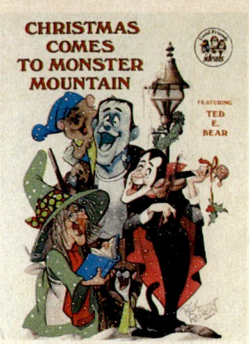

THE LITTLEST ANGEL is the delightful story of a small cherub who turns heaven upside down but who gives a special meaning to giving as he presents his most cherished possession to God's new Son. An enduring favorite. Hardcover.
32 pages   8-923 $3.25

CHRISTMAS COMES TO MONSTER MOUNTAIN features a popular Ideals' character, Ted E. Bear, narrating the story of how the world's most feared monsters find the warmth and spirit of Christmas. Accompanied by brilliant, full-color artwork by noted artist, Rick Reinert. Hardcover.
32 pages   8-024 $3.25

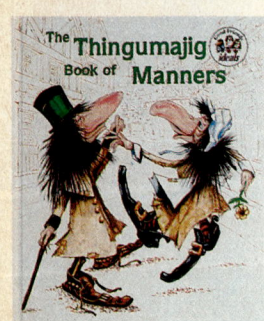

THINGUMAJIG BOOK OF MANNERS shows children fascinating creatures who behave disgracefully in public and in their own company! The scenes are accompanied with captions featuring the proper behavior in each situation. This book of un-manners is guaranteed to keep children away from bad habits! Hardcover.
32 pages   8-010 $3.25

THE BEAR WHO SLEPT THROUGH CHRISTMAS features the popular television hero, Ted E. Bear, who longs to celebrate Christmas in a special way. This heart-warming story will appeal to parents and children alike! Watch for Ted E. Bear on TV this season! Hardcover.
32 pages   8-942 $3.25

❄ C ❄ H ❄ I ❄ L ❄

LITTLE SLEEPYHEADS is a beautiful collection of favorite bedtime stories lovingly illustrated by Frances Hook. Enjoy such classics as "In the Land of Counterpane," "There Once Was a Puffin" and "One, Two, Buckle My Shoe."
32 pages   8-933 $1.95

ZIGGY AND HIS FRIENDS finds this favorite character bringing children the joy of music, color and companionship. Illustrated with full-color art, this book will be read again and again!
64 pages   8-939 $3.95

I'M THANKFUL EACH DAY portrays a child's heart-warmingly simple expression of gratitude for everything from apples to sunshine. Clever, full-color art accompanies the verse.
24 pages   8-008 $2.50

ONCE UPON A RHYME brings favorite nursery verses to life with delightful color artwork. "Sing a Song of Sixpence," "Little Boy Blue" and "To Market, To Market" are but a few of the rhymes to be enjoyed in this beautiful volume.
80 pages   8-055 $3.95

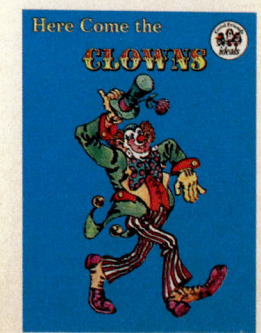

THAT'S WHAT A FRIEND IS describes for children the many facets of a close friendship . . . from bad times to good times. Accompanied by charming, color artwork.
32 pages   8-006 $2.50

HERE COME THE CLOWNS captures the antics of many different clowns in colorful, imaginative artwork. Humorous verses accompany this fascinating collection of characters.
32 pages   8-931 $1.95

BIBLE STORIES FOR CHILDREN brings the characters of the New Testament to life adding yet another dimension to children's most beloved Bible parables. Enchanting full-color art. Hardcover.
32 pages   8-017 $3.25

PRAYERS FOR CHILDREN captures the unique charm of favorite children's prayers. Whether before dinner or before bedtime, children will delight in repeating the classic verses. Features beautiful color artwork. Hardcover.
32 pages   8-023 $3.25

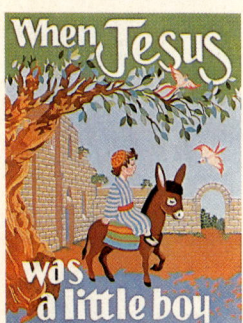

WHEN JESUS WAS A LITTLE BOY focuses on the childhood of Jesus. Children can readily identify with the little boy who does many of the same things they do in daily life. Lovely color art accompanies the verses.
32 pages   8-009 $2.50

STORY OF CHANUKAH FOR CHILDREN depicts the tale of the Jewish people's fight for religious freedom. The simple yet charming verses reveal the meanings behind some of the symbols of this important Jewish holiday, "The Festival of Lights." Full-color illustrations enhance the story.
32 pages   8-020 $2.50

D ❄ R ❄ E ❄ N ❄

COMMON SENSES is a beautifully illustrated collection of stories featuring five delightful animal characters who demonstrate just how important each of our five senses is. Rick Reinert's art brings the stories to life. Hardcover.
48 pages   8-022 $4.95

NEDOBECK'S NUMBERS BOOK makes learning numbers a thoroughly enjoyable experience for both youngsters and parents. Lovable, full color animal characters illustrate the verses. Hardcover.
32 pages   8-015 $3.25

IDEALS FOR KIDS is a special collection of favorite children's stories, poems and games. Brilliant color photography and artwork are sure to delight youngsters of all ages. It need not be a rainy day for children to find this volume entertaining!
64 pages   9-40 $3.95

NEDOBECK'S ALPHABET BOOK parades the fascinating characters of Don Nedobeck through the ABC's and gives letter learning a whole new appeal for both youngsters and parents. Full-color illustrations. Hardcover.
32 pages   8-016 $3.25

I CAN COOK COOKBOOK contains delicious recipes for the junior chef that the whole family will enjoy. Safety precautions plus step-by-step instructions ensure success for the beginning cook.
48 pages   8-935 $2.95

BIG BLUE MARBLE ATLAS is based on the popular television series for children. This colorful, deluxe edition is more than just a collection of maps: children learn of the culture and economic environment of the world's nations as well as their geography. Hardcover.
168 pages   8-924 $9.95

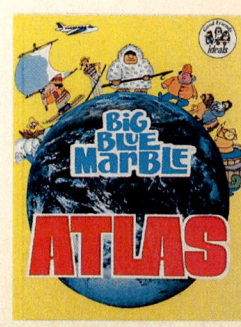

COOKIE COOKBOOK features over 200 tasty cookie recipes for sure-to-please family treats and holiday gift-giving. Sixteen color photographs, baking and mailing tips and a list of substitutions accompany the text.
64 pages   3-639 $2.95

NICE AND EASY DESSERTS COOKBOOK is an outstanding collection of fabulous desserts accompanied by a selection of brilliant color photographs. You're sure to find many delights ranging from crunchy cookies to fabulous tortes!
64 pages   3-612 $2.95

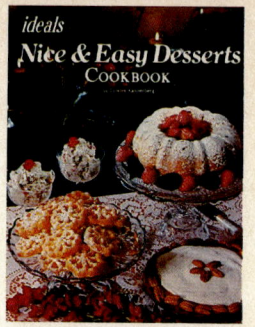

CANDY COOKBOOK contains taste-tempting recipes for all types of candy, including a dietetic section. A comprehensive introduction makes it possible for even the beginner to prepare beautiful gifts this holiday season!
64 pages   3-615 $2.95

GOURMET APPETIZER COOKBOOK is a superb collection of easy, delicious recipes for hot and cold appetizers to tempt both the cook and her guests. Perfect for year round entertaining as well as festive holiday occasions. Beautiful color photographs illustrate the chapters.
64 pages   3-618 $2.95

COOKBOOKS

MEXICAN COOKBOOK contains recipes gleaned from a diverse and exciting cuisine. Featured is a short history of Mexican cooking, information on the types of ingredients used and a glossary. Chapters range from Antojitos to Postre (Appetizers to Desserts).
64 pages   3-000 $2.95

LOW CALORIE COOKBOOK incorporates tips of how to cut calories in everyday cooking while highlighting flavor and eye appeal in dishes the whole family will enjoy. Each recipe gives the calorie content per serving. Features recipes such as Rock Lobster Continental, Veal Scallopini with Mushrooms and Blueberry-Banana Bread.
64 pages   3-003 $2.95

SOUP, SALAD, SANDWICH COOKBOOK has over 200 tempting recipes for what usually is thought to be ordinary fare. This delightful collection is accompanied with brilliant color photographs and serving suggestions.
64 pages   3-001 $2.95

COOKING FOR TWO COOKBOOK is designed to meet the needs of those who are buying and preparing foods for just two people. The amount of protein, fat and carbohydrate for each recipe is given. Included are superb selections such as Turbot de Joie, Italian Quiche and Bacon Crescent Rolls.
64 pages   3-004 $2.95

CHINESE COOKBOOK is an introduction to Chinese cooking that makes learning fun as well as easy. Included are methods of cooking, a glossary of common terms, an introduction to basic cutting methods and types of cuisine such as Szechuan and Cantonese.
64 pages   3-002 $2.95

GROUND MEAT COOKBOOK will show you how to use your culinary talents to make delicious fare out of various types of ground meat. These taste-tempting recipes use a cut of meat to full advantage and are easy on the budget.
64 pages   3-005 $2.95

Dear Friend,

A few months ago, Ideals announced the acquisition of Structures Publishing Company, a leader in the publication of home improvement books.

We are pleased to present 6 newly published titles, listed below. The same high quality that Ideals has been noted for through the years is present in this new Successful Home Improvement Series.

In addition, we are also offering a comprehensive book that is an established leader in the Structures line. HOW TO BUILD YOUR OWN HOME is indispensible to those who wish to be directly involved in or supervise the construction of their dwelling.

Individually or as a complete set, these volumes provide an excellent resource for those homeowners interested in saving time and money in home repair and planning. Perseverance and our new books are all you need for success in your home improvement projects!

HOW TO BUILD YOUR OWN HOME

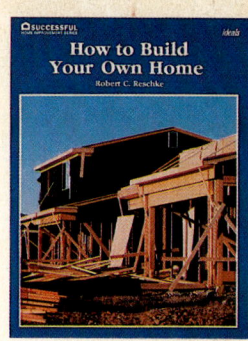

HOW TO BUILD YOUR OWN HOME encompasses every detail of home construction, whether you are actually building your own dwelling or dealing with architects, contractors and/or builders. In 50 detailed chapters, the homeowner will find topics from financing and choosing the site to finishing the driveway and landscaping. Over 600 photographs, drawings, charts and diagrams accompany the text.
352 pages   6-112 $9.95

SUCCESSFUL HOME IMPROVEMENT SERIES

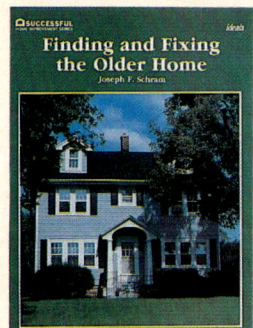

FINDING AND FIXING THE OLDER HOME contains guidelines on what to look for in an older home, such as structural and cosmetic strengths and weaknesses and how much time and money should be invested over and above the purchase price to bring the dwelling up to current standards. Basic instructions for repairing and remodeling both the interior and exterior are included.
96 pages   6-110 $3.95

KITCHEN PLANNING AND REMODELING offers a comprehensive selection of ideas for helping the homeowner modernize the kitchen to be efficient and workable in the available space. The easy-to-follow instructions cover all aspects of kitchen improvement: planning and design for specific needs or interests, color use, lighting, ventilation, counters and sinks, cabinets and space-saving ideas and energy-saving devices.
96 pages   6-103 $3.95

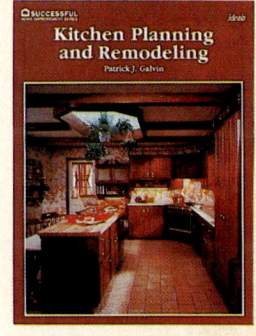

MONEY SAVING HOME REPAIR GUIDE features clear, detailed instructions and diagrams to enable the average homeowner, with little or no experience, to handle almost any repair without the services of a contractor. Homeowners will be able to repair squeaking and sagging floors, cracked walls, and ceilings, plumbing problems, damaged roofs, windows and doors and basic electrical problems.
96 pages   6-100 $3.95

HOME PLANS FOR THE 80's contains designs for 188 homes, featuring exterior renderings and complete floor plans. Types of plans presented include: Tudor, Early Colonial, French, Spanish and Contemporary. Special sections include: vacation homes and low/medium cost homes. Sources for the specific plans are listed.
96 pages   6-109 $3.95

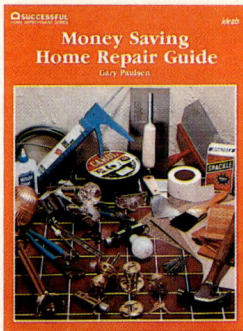

SHELVES AND BUILT-INS is the answer for the homeowner at wits' end for lack of ample storage space. It provides step-by-step instructions and construction details for building shelves, counters, cabinets, bookcases and storage units. Information on how to work with various materials is provided along with specific projects such as kitchen cabinets, bathroom vanities, room dividers and closets.
96 pages   6-104 $3.95

BATHROOM PLANNING AND REMODELING contains easy-to-follow instructions enabling the homeowner to undertake any type of bathroom remodeling with ease and confidence. Whether you are planning and designing a new bathroom or improving and remodeling an existing one, you will find a wealth of ideas among the beautiful contemporary and traditional plans and styles in this volume.
96 pages   6-102 $3.95

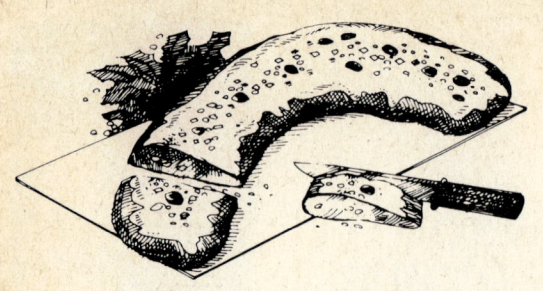

How much does $1.00 buy today?

At the service station, barely enough to get your car home—at the grocery store, hardly enough to put in a bag. That's what makes this SPECIAL $1.00 OFFER from Ideals so exciting!

Just complete the order card (attached) and send it with $1.00 for your introduction to the IDEALS COUNTRY KITCHEN PLAN. We'll rush you 2 regular editions of Ideals Cookbooks (Nice and Easy Desserts and Country Kitchen) and a FREE BONUS recipe card collection.....a $6.90 retail value.....all for just $1.00!!!

• NO HIDDEN CHARGES • NO CLUB TO JOIN • CANCEL ANYTIME •
• NO POSTAGE & HANDLING FEES • NO SALES TAX •

After receiving your introductory shipment, you will receive 2 new cookbooks each month for the next 3 months . . . and you pay only $5.00 for each shipment!

The 5th shipment will complete your collection. You can pay for these 18 cookbooks in the month received and earn a SPECIAL DISCOUNT . . . or simply pay $5.00 that month and $5.00 per month for the next 8 months. Many of our readers call this the "pay as you cook plan." But there is more . . . with the 5th shipment, we will send you a handsome LUCITE COOKBOOK VIEWER (a $6.95 value) . . . ABSOLUTELY FREE!

The 26 books in this collection are listed on the following page. Perhaps you may see some books that you've already purchased. If that is the case, you know how great they are. Others participating in this plan who have found similar "duplicates" use these additional copies as wonderful gifts. Remember each book costs you $2.50 or less!

START YOUR COLLECTION TODAY!

• You can mail your card and payment in the envelope with your catalog order—but this offer does not apply toward the FREE GIFT offer for catalog purchases.

• Sorry, but we cannot process gift orders—the collection must be sent to the same address that will pay for the shipment.

• Fill out the card and place it along with $1.00 in an envelope TODAY! (We recommend a check or money order.)

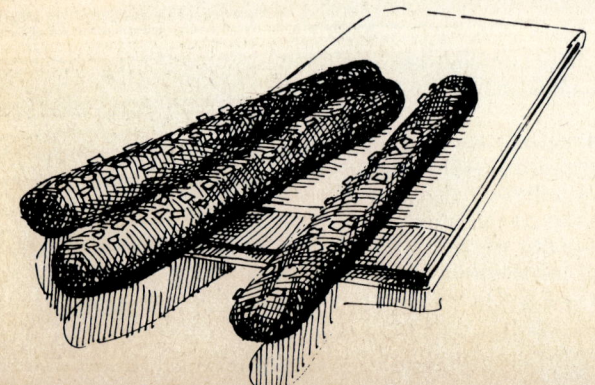

ideals Country Kitchen Plan

Send for 2 REGULAR EDITION COOKBOOKS

PLUS a FREE recipe card collection

all for only $1.00

A TOTAL RETAIL VALUE $6.90

you are then entitled to obtain 24 additional cookbooks . . . all at a Discount

PLUS receive absolutely free this practical lucite cookbook stand with your final shipment!

Meatless Meals
Fish & Seafood
Country Bread
Soups for All Seasons
Budget Saving Meals
Mama's Kitchen
Easy Cake Decorating
Tempting Treasures
Christmas Kitchen
Gourmet Appetizer
Mama D's Italian
Chicken & Poultry
Gourmet on the Go
Naturally Nutritious
Gourmet Christmas
Mama's Honey Jar
Gourmet Touch
Menus from Around the World
Family
Cookie
Candy
Barbecue
Farmhouse
Microwave
Nice & Easy Desserts
Country Kitchen

Receive 2 Cookbooks and a FREE Recipe Card Collection for only $1.00. Receive 2 new Cookbooks at a special discount price of $2.50 each in months 2, 3 & 4. In month 5, receive 18 new Cookbooks. Pay only $5.00 per month for 9 months — or pay entire balance in month received and earn a Special Discount!

NO CLUB TO JOIN • NO HIDDEN FEES • CANCEL ANYTIME

Friendship is made of God's beautiful things: it is the music that makes our hearts sing, the sunshine that lights up our lives each day, the flowers that bloom all along life's way.

Hearts that know friendship are ones truly blessed, for friendship is love and brings happiness. It is woven through time and always will bring a happy today and tomorrows that sing.

Joy of Friendship
Vera Hardman

A Legacy of Laughter

Sometimes when I read of great men leaving vast fortunes to their heirs, I smile to myself. My own dad was a great man. Yet the legacy he left was not in tangible "things." It was far greater than jewels or wealth. The legacy my dad left was the legacy of laughter.

I was born during the Depression, when times were not just hard, they were almost impossible. We lived on a little farm outside a logging community in northwestern Washington State. It was a "sunup to sundown" existence. Mom trotted to get more done. Dad kept the farm and worked every other job he could find, and there were precious few of them! We had enough to eat and wear, but at times there wasn't even a postage stamp to send a letter—and stamps only cost two cents. Some years they made fifty dollars, if they were lucky, which went for salt, sugar, and other things we couldn't raise.

It was grim and hard, no time for joy and gladness. Yet in our home, the Depression was something for others. We never considered ourselves poor; poor people had less than we did! The difference was—we laughed. From early childhood, no matter how bad things were, we laughed—cleansing, healing laughter, often chasing away the tears. We ended childhood arguments with a laugh. When we didn't have money to go places, we stayed home, did something else, and laughed.

The Depression ended, only to be followed by World War II. There wasn't much laughter in the world then. There was anguish, friends and loved ones in the service. Yet in spite of our sorrows, we still laughed. When there was no sugar for cookies and candy, Mom popped corn, or made "doughgods," funny little pieces of dough fried directly on the well-scrubbed kitchen range. In winter we curled up by the light of kerosene lamps, reading our books. In summer we ran through woods, played our games, and eventually flopped to the ground, to look at cloud pictures and laugh.

The day the war ended everyone laughed. People shouted, wildly making sure everyone knew the good news—we were free!

Years passed. There was more money for such things as camping trips, things that held families together. There were walks to the river, fishing trips, cookouts, all invisibly binding us together with memories. Our laughter rang golden as the sunlight, warm as the campfires. We laughed at the dog, the cats, ourselves, each other. We laughed because we were alive. Season followed season; we still laughed.

My older brother became of service age during the Korean conflict. He was fortunate. He was sent to Japan. He came home with funny tales of a different way of life, how he felt big and powerful next to the smaller Japanese race. We loved it all—and laughed.

As time passed and the boys married, the family scattered. Yet our family reunions were times of joy, gladness, and laughter.

About then a little eight-year-old boy came to live with Dad, Mom and me. He was a solemn little fellow, all big eyes, who huddled close to Mom. Not for long. Dad taught him to laugh, just as the rest of us had been taught. Soon we were laughing at Jerry's antics, from getting stuck in the rainbarrel under the eaves to sliding off the snow-covered roof and landing upside-down in a snowbank.

Our biggest test was yet to come. Dad hadn't been feeling well. It was the summer of 1968. We took him to the hospital, teased him, and shaved him with a new electric razor on Saturday. Sunday night he took a turn for the worse and died the next morning quietly, as he had lived, and with dignity.

The funeral was over, and by the time we reached home, the heavens were black. Wild storm clouds gathered; the rain poured. My two brothers and I stood numbly on the covered back porch, watching the storm, just as we had watched many storms before.

Bang! Crash! Boom! What a wild day it was! It snatched from me words I'd have held back if I'd only stopped to think. I looked up into those tumultuous heavens and said, "Would you believe it? Dad's just gotten up there, and already he's throwing a big party!" My brothers stared. Then it came. Laughter louder than thunder, mingled with tears the size of the spattering raindrops. Dad's legacy to us—the laughter that would heal, console, and allow us to go on.

Years have passed, many of them. Yet when I stand watching a storm, for a moment I am back in the old homeplace, watching the storms of life as well as the weather. I am hearing again the hearty laughter of a dad who had learned to ride the swells of those storms.

He never made a lot of money. He never held a high office. He never claimed to be anything except what he was—a man who loved his family. But Dad's gift to his children can never be lost.

What is the measure of a man except what he gives those who follow? They will inevitably find themselves influenced by those winding ruts he has created.

There are many things a man can leave his heirs, but few will ever match the legacy of laughter my dad gave his children.

Colleen L. Reece

River Bend

Bright clouds, tall firs
   And pines lie upside down
     Upon the mirror
       Of the river bend;

    While distant blue green
     Beauty leans against
       The curve where
         Shining sand and water blend.

   In sheltered coves
     The little ripples weave
       Small lengths of rich moire;
     But in the wide

      Majestic current,
       Deep and powerful,
         There seems no movement
           To the mighty stride.

No voice of man or beast
   Disturbs the peace.
   Whole benediction
     Lingers like a psalm

    Upon the green
     And crystal autograph
       Which God pens here,
        In solitude and calm.

           Jessie Wilmore Murton

Autumn

Today the peace of autumn pervades the world.

In the radiant noon, silent and motionless, the wide stillness rests like a tired bird spreading, over the deserted fields to all horizons, its wings of golden green.

Today the thin thread of the river flows without song, leaving no mark on its sandy banks.

The many distant villages bask in the sun with eyes closed in idle and languid slumber.

In the stillness I hear in every blade of grass, in every speck of dust, in every part of my own body, in the visible and invisible worlds, in the planets, the sun, and the stars, the joyous dance of the atoms through endless time—the myriad murmuring waves of rhythm surrounding Thy throne.

Rabindranath Tagore

American Sunset

Crimson ripples on the sea,
As evening's globe of fire descends,
Please the weary fisher's eyes
As homeward bound his small ship wends.

Cowboys pause atop the mesa
To feast their eyes on sunset's glory;
Many days thus close in beauty,
A lovely end to daytime's story.

    Distant tractors now stand silent
    With windrowed harvest nigh;
    Farmers turn their faces westward
    Where heavens paint their evening sky.

        No other land can match her glory,
        None blessed with such abundant love
        In freedom, pride and love of country;
        We lift our eyes to God above.

            Early twilight church bells pealing
            Bring the Christians forth in prayer,
            Basking in America's freedom,
            Thankful for the Master's care.

                    Emily Scarlett

A Thanksgiving Day Prayer

O Lord, with humble hearts we pray
Thy blessing this Thanksgiving Day
And ask that at each table place,
Where grateful folk say words of grace,
That Thou will come to share the yield
Thy bounty gave to farm and field.
We pray Thy love will bless, O Lord,
Each hearth, each home, each festive board;
And that Thy peace will come to stay
When candles glow, Thanksgiving Day.

Brian F. King

The miracle of autumn brings
Again the filled bin;
The season's harvest days are done;
The year's full yield is in.
Filled is every space and storehouse
With enough to spare,
A bounteous gift of Providence,
A benevolence to share.

Autumn Harvest

Give thanks to the Provider,
Each in his native tongue,
All creeds and races, rich and poor,
The aged and the young,
For fields to till, crops to gather,
All across this spacious land,
Prized possessions all of which
God lends a helping hand.

On this day set aside give thanks
In quietness serene
For a world of wondrous beauty,
For changes yet unseen.
Give thanks for the togetherness
Of family and friends,
For time and opportunity,
And faith that never ends.

Abigail Falk

Thanksgiving

There dawned a frosty morning
In the autumn of the year,
When the crops had all been gathered,
And the air was crisp and clear.

The Pilgrims all rose early
To lend a helping hand
And lay a festive table
With the bounty of the land.

Soon the farmers from the harvest
And the hunters from the wood
Brought the pumpkins and the turkeys
And the ripened fruits they could.

Then the Pilgrims paused a moment,
To bow their heads and pray,
And thanked God for His blessings
On that first Thanksgiving Day.

Jean M. Helferich

Give the Poor Persimmon a Break

Persimmons are a neglected fruit, yet they have an elegant flavor and great possibilities. Granted, they are not the most beautiful fruit and will pucker your mouth if eaten before they have ripened. Try persimmons in the fall, when they are available in the market produce section. They are delicious in cookies, pudding, salads, ice cream and bread.

In America, persimmons date back to the days of early explorers. DeSoto reported the presence of persimmons in the southern United States in the 1540s. Jan deLaet described the persimmon in his writings about Virginia in 1558. Persimmons were used by Indians as food and by early settlers in the Appalachian and Ozark highlands for persimmon bread, supposedly superior to gingerbread. The seeds, when roasted or ground, are used as a coffee substitute in the southern United States. The green fruit contains tannic acid and is used as a domestic remedy for diarrhea and chronic dysentery. Persimmons are a source of vitamins A and C.

In the United States, there are two principal varieties of persimmons: the Oriental and the native American. The Oriental (native to central and northern China) grows primarily in the western states, California in particular. The native American variety can be found in the southern and eastern parts of the United States.

The Oriental variety (D. kaki) resembles a tomato in size and shape. The fruit may be up to three inches in diameter and is bright yellow to orange when ripe. If eaten before it is soft-ripe, it is unpleasantly astringent.

The native American persimmon tree (Diospyros, species D. virginiana), elegant and wide-spreading may grow to seventy-five feet. The deep root system adapts to a wide range of soils. The fruit is triangular in shape, about three inches in diameter. It must be ripened by a hard frost which softens it, removing the astringency and developing a rich flavor. In the southern part of the United States, this variety is often found along fencerows around fields.

Either variety of persimmon may be frozen. To freeze, peel and place the whole fruit in a blender for pureeing. After blending, the pulp may be frozen by cupfuls in plastic bags. This frozen pulp keeps from one season to another without losing flavor.

If you wish to dry the whole fruit, the Hachiya, a variety of Oriental, is best. Peel the fruit while it is still firm and yet bright orange in color; do not cut up. Hang the fruit by the stem using a durable string or plastic cord. Be certain the area in which the fruit hangs is dry. After it has hung for several days, break up the fibers by lightly kneading the fruit. Continue doing this over the several weeks it takes to completely dry the persimmons. When ready to eat, the persimmon is wrinkled and resembles a prune.

In California, the Fuyu variety (Oriental) is popular for slicing and drying. Wash but do not peel the persimmons. Cut into 3/8-inch slices. Place in single layers on trays. Dry for 14 to 18 hours until hard, but still bendable. To reconstitute, place ½ cup of persimmon slices in a narrow, high-walled container so ½ cup of warm water will almost cover them. Soak overnight until soft. Eat as fresh.

Dried persimmons may be used in recipes without soaking if they are pureed in a blender with water.

Persimmon Cookies

Makes 3 dozen cookies.

- 1 cup persimmon pulp
- 1 teaspoon baking soda
- 1 cup sugar
- ½ cup shortening
- 1 egg
- 2 cups flour
- 1 teaspoon ground cinnamon
- ½ teaspoon each ground cloves, nutmeg and salt
- 1 cup raisins (dates or dried prunes)
- 1 cup chopped walnuts (or pecans)

Use electric mixer to beat persimmon pulp with baking soda, sugar and shortening until creamy. Add egg, flour, spices, raisins and nuts. Drop by spoonfuls onto greased cookie sheet. Bake at 350° from 12 to 15 minutes.

Note: The same ingredients may be used, the mixture poured into a greased and floured 10 x 15-inch pan and baked at 350° for 50 minutes. Cool on a rack for 5 minutes. Spread top with a lemon glaze made by mixing 1 cup confectioners' sugar and 2 tablespoons lemon juice. When cool, cut into bars.

Persimmon Salad

Makes 8 servings.

- 1 3-ounce package each of lemon- and orange-flavored gelatin
- 1 small can crushed pineapple, drained reserve juice
- 3 large ripe persimmons

Add 2 cups of boiling water to the gelatin and dissolve thoroughly. To the reserved pineapple juice add sufficient water to make 1½ cups of liquid. Add a dash of salt. Cool till slightly thickened, then fold fruit into the mixture and refrigerate until time to serve.

Persimmon Fruitcake

Makes 2 loaves.

- 1¼ cups persimmon pulp
- 2 teaspoons baking soda
- 1 cup each brown and white sugar
- ¾ cup shortening
- 2 eggs
- 2½ cups flour
- 2 teaspoons ground cinnamon
- 1 teaspoon each salt, ground nutmeg and cloves
- 3 tablespoons white vinegar
- 1 jar candied fruit mix
- 1 cup raisins (plumped in hot water)
- 1 cup chopped nuts

Mix persimmon pulp, soda, sugars and shortening until well blended. Add eggs and beat well. Add dry ingredients alternately to the mixture with vinegar. Mix in the fruit and nuts. Pour into 2 greased and floured loaf pans. Bake at 350° for 1½ hours.

Persimmon Ice Cream

Makes about 3 cups.

- 1 cup sliced dried persimmons
- 1 cup water
- ¼ teaspoon ground cinnamon
- ⅛ teaspoon each ground cloves and mace
- 2½ tablespoons fresh lemon juice
- 2 cups vanilla ice cream, softened

Combine the first 5 ingredients in a blender until the mixture is the consistency of a thick sauce. Add lemon juice as needed. Pour the mixture over ice cream in a bowl and stir to blend. Place in freezing trays until firm.

Actually, the persimmon tree can claim good looks all year round. Neatly tailored leaves emerge in the spring and turn color in the fall; an interesting bare-branch pattern is visible in winter. Even the bark, with its checkerboard pattern, has a pleasing texture. The fruit hangs like Christmas ornaments for a number of weeks in the fall.

Even if you are not fortunate enough to have a persimmon tree yourself, don't shy away from the fruit in the produce section of your market. Make a resolution that this season you will at least try persimmons—sliced raw like apples, or in cookies, cake, or whatever use appeals to you. You may become a convert!

Mildred Estes

Homage to November

Sing praise to November!
The farmer's harvest safe
within the bulging bin and mow;
the jelly ruby in the jar;
the garden produce proudly counted
in the quart, the pint, the frozen box;
the leaf fall finished
and the migrant birds all flown.
Now watch the sun rise later
and fall earlier to darkness
in late November afternoon.

Now take time to savor
the aftermath of harvest,
to cheer the football hero,
and to think again of Pilgrim folk
sharing the fruits of their new world
with Indian brothers and giving thanks
for the richness of this land.
Sing praise to November!
      Elizabeth Searle Lamb

How We Kept Thanksgiving at Oldtown

Abridged from Harriet Beecher Stowe's novel *Oldtown Folks*

Scott Giantvalley

People have often supposed, because the Puritans founded a society where there were no professed public amusements, that there was no fun going on, and that there were no cakes and ale, because Puritans were so virtuous. They were never more mistaken in their lives. There was an abundance of sober, well-considered merriment; but the king of all festivals was the autumn Thanksgiving.

When the apples were all gathered, the cider was all made, the yellow pumpkins were rolled in, the corn was husked, the labors of the season were done, and the warm, late days of Indian summer came in, dreamy and calm and still, with just enough frost to crisp the ground of a morning, but with warm traces of benign, sunny hours at noon, there came over the community a sort of genial repose of spirit, a sense of something accomplished, and of a new golden mark made on the calendar of life. The deacon began to say to the minister, of a Sunday, "I suppose it's about time for the Thanksgiving proclamation."

We felt its approach in all departments of the household, the conversation at this time beginning to turn to high and solemn culinary mysteries and receipts of wondrous power and virtue.

For as much as a week beforehand, we children were employed in chopping mince for pies to a most wearisome fineness and in pounding cinnamon, allspice, and cloves in a great mortar; and the sound of its pounding and chopping reechoed through all the rafters of the old house with a hearty and vigorous cheer, most refreshing to our spirits.

In those days there were none of the thousand ameliorations of the labors of housekeeping which have since arisen—no ground and prepared spices and sweet herbs; everything came into our hands in the rough, and in bulk, and the reducing of it into a state for use was deemed one of the appropriate labors of childhood.

At other times of the year we sometimes murmured at these labors, but those that were supposed to usher in the great Thanksgiving festival were always entered into with enthusiasm. There were signs of richness all around us: stoning of raisins, cutting of citron, slicing of candied orange peel. Yet all these were only dawnings and intimations of what was coming during the week of real preparation, after the governor's proclamation had been read.

The glories of that proclamation! We knew beforehand the Sunday it was to be read, and the cheering anticipation sustained us through what seemed to us the long waste of the sermon and prayers. When at last the auspicious moment approached, we children poked one another, and fairly giggled with unreproved delight as we listened to the crackle of the slowly unfolding document. That great sheet of paper impressed us as something supernatural, by reason of its mighty size, and by the broad seal of the state affixed thereto; and when the minister read, "By his excellency, the governor of the Commonwealth of Massachusetts, a proclamation . . . ," our mirth was with difficulty repressed by admonitory glances from our sympathetic elders. Then, after a solemn enumeration of the benefits which the commonwealth had that year received at the hands of Divine Providence, came at last the naming of the eventful day. And now came on the week in earnest!

The making of pies at this period assumed vast proportions that verged upon the sublime. Pies were made by forties and fifties and hundreds, and made of everything on the earth and under the earth.

The pie is an English institution, which, planted on American soil, forthwith ran rampant and burst forth into an untold variety of genera and species. Not merely the old traditional mince pie, but a thousand strictly American seedlings from that main stock, evinced the power of American housewives to adapt old institutions to new uses. Pumpkin pies, cranberry pies, huckleberry pies, cherry pies, green currant pies, peach, pear, and plum pies, custard pies, apple pies, Marlborough-pudding pies—pies with top crusts and pies without, pies adorned with all sorts of fanciful flutings and architectural strips laid across and around, and otherwise varied—attested the boundless fertility of the feminine mind, when once let loose in a given direction.

In the corner of the great kitchen, during all those days, the jolly old oven roared and crackled in great volcanic billows of flame, snapping and gurgling as if the old fellow entered with joyful sympathy into the frolic of the hour; and then, his great heart being once warmed up, he brooded over successive generations of pies and cakes, which went in raw and came out cooked, till butteries, dressers, shelves and pantries were literally crowded with a jostling abundance.

During this eventful preparation week, all the female part of my grandmother's household were at a height above any ordinary state of mind; they moved about the house rapt in a species of prophetic frenzy. It seemed to be considered a necessary feature of such festivals, that everybody should be in a hurry, and everything in the house should be turned bottom upwards with enthusiasm; so at least we children understood it, and we certainly did our part to keep the ball rolling.

Well, at last, when all the chopping and pounding and baking and brewing, preparatory to the festival, were gone through with, the eventful day dawned. Great as the preparations were for the dinner, everything was so contrived that not a soul in the house should be kept from the morning service of Thanksgiving in the church and from listening to the Thanksgiving sermon. But it is to be confessed, that, when the good minister got carried away by the enthusiasm of his subject to extend these exercises beyond a certain length, anxious glances exchanged between good wives sometimes indicated a weakness of the flesh, having a tender reference to the turkeys and chickens and chicken pies, which might possibly be overdoing in the ovens at home. But the old brick oven was a true Puritan institution, backed up by the devotional habits of good housewives, that took capital care of whatever was committed to its capacious bosom. A truly well-bred oven would have been ashamed of itself and blushed redder than its own fires, if a God-fearing housewife, away at the temple of the Lord, should come home and find her piecrust either burned or underdone; so it generally managed to bring things out exactly right.

When sermons and prayers were all over, we children rushed home to see the great feast of the year spread.

What chitterings and chatterings there were all over the house, as all the aunties and uncles and cousins came pouring in, taking off their things, looking at one another's bonnets and dresses, and mingling their comments on the morning sermon with various opinions on the new millinery outfits, and with bits of home news, and kindly neighborhood gossip.

Who shall do justice to the dinner and describe the turkey, chickens, and chicken pies with all that endless variety of vegetables which the American soil and climate have contributed to the table and which, without regard to the French doctrine of courses, were all piled together in jovial abundance upon the board? There was much carving, laughing, talking and eating; and all showed that cheerful ability to dispatch the provisions which was the ruling spirit of the hour. After the meat came the plum puddings, and then the endless array of pies, till human nature was actually bewildered and overpowered by the tempting variety; and even we children turned from the profusion offered to us and wondered what was the matter that we could eat no more.

When all was over, my grandfather rose at the head of the table, and a fine venerable picture he made as he stood there, his silver hair flowing in curls down each side of his clear, calm face, while, in conformity to the old Puritan custom, he called attention to a recital of the mercies of God in his dealings with the family; and then he gave out that psalm which in those days might be called the national hymn of the Puritans.

And now, the dinner being cleared away, we youngsters, already excited to a tumult of laughter, tumbled into the best room for a game of blindman's buff, while the elderly women washed up the dishes and got the house in order, and the men folks went out to the barn, looked at the cattle, walked over the farm and talked of the crops.

In the evening the house was all open and lighted with the best of tallow candles; it was understood that we were to have a dance, and the musician had rosined his bow and tuned his fiddle.

Whenever or wherever it was that the idea of the sinfulness of dancing arose in New England, I know not; it is a certain fact that at Oldtown, at this time, the presence of the minister and his lady was held not to be in the slightest degree incompatible with this amusement. Of course the dances in those days were of a strictly moral nature. The very thought of one of the dances of modern times would have sent Lady Lothrop behind her big fan in helpless confusion and exploded my grandmother like a full-charged arsenal of indignation. As it was, she stood, her broad pleased face radiant with satisfaction, as the wave of joyousness crept up higher and higher round her, till the elders, who stood keeping time with their heads and feet, began to tell one another how they had danced with their sweethearts in good old days gone by; and the elder women began to blush and boast of steps that they could take in their youth, till the music finally subdued them, and into the dance they went.

"Well, well!" said my grandmother, "they're all at it so hearty, I don't see why I shouldn't try it myself." And into the Virginia reel she went, amid screams of laughter from all the younger members of the company.

But I assure you my grandmother was not a woman to be laughed at; for whatever she once started, she continued with a sturdy energy befitting a daughter of the Puritans.

"Why shouldn't I dance?" she asked, when she arrived red and resplendent at the bottom of the set. "Didn't Mr. Despondency and Miss Muchafraid and Mr. Readytohalt all dance together in the Pilgrim's Progress?" The minister in his ample flowing wig and his lady in her stiff brocade gave my grandmother a solemn twinkle of approbation.

As nine o'clock struck, the whole scene dissolved and melted; for what well-regulated village would think of carrying festivities beyond that hour?

And so ended our Thanksgiving at Oldtown.

Autumn's Golden Hour

Walk quietly here—
Lest birds be stirred to flight
By sound of feet
Upon the russet leaves
Along the garden path.

Walk slowly—
Lest you miss the beauty
Of this golden hour
That soon will purple
Beneath autumn skies.

Walk gently—
While life becomes imbued
With nature's riches,
And hopes that once were only dreams
Lie warm upon the heart.

May Smith White

A Hymn for the Harvest of 1847

AMERICAN

O nation, Christian nation,
Lift high the hymn of praise;
The God of our salvation
Is love in all His ways;
He blesseth us and feedeth
Ev'ry creature of His hand,
To succor him that needeth
And gladden all the land—
To succor him that needeth
And gladden all the land.

Rejoice, ye happy people!
And peal the changing chime,
From every belfried steeple
In symphony sublime;
Let cottage and let palace
Be thankful and rejoice;
And woods, and hills, and valleys
Reecho the glad voice.

From glen, and plain, and city
Let gracious incense rise;
The Lord of Life in pity
Hath heard His creatures' cries;
And where, in fierce oppressing,
Stalked fever, fear, and dearth,
He pours a triple blessing
To fill and fatten earth!

Composed
for the
Thanksgiving
Day

Words by the Author of
"Proverbial Philosophy"

HOMESTEAD AUTUMN
Currier and Ives

Gaze round in deep emotion;
The rich and ripened grain
Is like a golden ocean
Becalmed upon the plain;
And we, who late were weepers,
Lest judgment should destroy,
Now sing, because the reapers
Are come again with joy!

O praise the hand that giveth—
And giveth evermore—
To every soul that liveth
Abundance flowing o'er!
For every soul he filleth
With manna from above
And over all distilleth
The unction of His love.

Then gather, Christians, gather,
To praise with heart and voice
The good Almighty Father,
Who biddeth you rejoice;
For He hath turned the sadness
Of His children into mirth,
And we will sing with gladness
The harvest home of earth!

Let your heart be open
    as a field.
Let it contain a myriad
    of life,
Of grasses and weeds,
    birds, insects and small animals,
Of sun, wind, rain,
    fertile earth nourished sweetly.
Let this be the knowledge
    of your heart—
To guide an opening
    of your mind's eye,
To see, understand
    and feel
Life, as it is vibrant
    to be.

Vibrant

Shari Style

Thanksgiving Tapestry

Special Thoughts about Thanksgiving

Harvest

This the proof of God's provision:
Faith has known each tiny seed,
Bringing forth the fruit in season;
Love has met man's every need.

J. Evans Anderson

Count Your Blessings

Thanksgiving comes to us each year.
Some pray, some feast, some rest.
I fold my hands and bow my head
And count the ways I'm blest.

Lucille Crumley

Thanks and Love

We have many things to be thankful for;
Many blessings the Lord has sent.
Let us give thanks on this Thanksgiving Day,
Keep love as a daily event.

Raymond W. Eberhardt

This Day of Cheer

As we look up and thank the Lord
For peace again this year,
Let's give Him thanks for people
Who brought this day of cheer.

D.A. Hoover

Dear Father

In Heaven, for Your tender care, for our food, and home, and loved ones, too, we bow our heads to honor You. From deep in our hearts comes this thankful prayer for all that we have, because we know life would be graceless without Your glow.

Amen

Patricia Clafford

Stubble

I like a field of stubble where the wheat
Is in the shock and heavy with its yield,
For then the earth seems resting and replete
With peace; and yet there plainly is revealed
In some strange manner by the quiet soil
That man has gained reward for faith and toil.

Margaret E. Brune

Autumn ... the year's last, loveliest smile.
William Cullen Bryant

Autumn

The morns are meeker than they were;
The nuts are getting brown.
The berry's cheek is plumper;
The rose is out of town.

The maple wears a gayer scarf,
The field a scarlet gown.
Lest I should be old-fashioned,
I'll put a trinket on.
Emily Dickinson

I Heard God's Voice

I heard God's voice in a field of wheat
Where heads in grateful homage bent
Before a whispering breeze that passed,
Confiding its deep content.

A field sparrow piped his solo there
In praise of his Maker wise and good;
God's voice spoke out of that golden sea—
I listened where I stood.
Cecile Houghton Stury

Let Us Give Thanks

Did you ever notice what a warm glow real thankfulness imparts, both to the giver and to the receiver? All of us have so much to be thankful for in this life, that we surely should be happy most of the time. In this season of Thanksgiving, let us count up our personal blessings, material and intangible, and give, from overflowing hearts, that gratitude which we owe to God and our fellow men.
Esther Baldwin York

Gather In the Harvest

As we gather in the harvest,
Lord, we thank Thee for the yield
Of heavily laden fruit trees
And of every bounteous field.
Now is the time of plenty
As we fill the cellar and haymow.
Each bin is overflowing;
Dear Lord, we thank Thee now.
Thelma Hice Moeller

Autumn

Autumn wears an amber gown
Of taffeta and lace,
That rustles like the dying leaves
She forces out of place.
Linda Lowe

Thankful Hearts

Now our hearts are truly thankful
As we view the blessings given,
And we breathe a deep thanksgiving
To our Father, God in Heaven.
Addie Lincoln Jones

Thanksgiving Day

Thanksgiving Day has come again;
We bow our heads in prayer
And thank God for His blessings
And His love that's everywhere.
Isla Paschal Richardson

Autumn Trail

Caroline Henning Bair

Come, walk with me along the autumn trails
    When sails
Of milkweed floss are floating on the breeze,
And sumacs lift their gorgeous plumes of red;
    While overhead
The wild grape clusters hang from moss-grown trees.

We'll linger by a quiet sylvan stream
    To dream,
Where pheasants play among the goldenrod,
And build our life anew and leave our cares
    All unawares
Among the purple aster blooms with God.

When sunset's flaming fires are burning low,
    We'll go
Back to the homestead where our loved ones wait
To welcome us, as stars appear to light
    The night,
And twilight softly fades beyond the gate.

North Woods Notebook
Thanksgiving Dinner Was Seventeen Miles Away

My husband, Bob, was the youngest of ten children born to Comb and Anna Andersen Bourgeois. The family lived in Park Falls, Wisconsin, when Bob was born on August 20, 1923; during his childhood there were several moves to farms and small towns throughout northern Wisconsin.

Bob's memories of his childhood remain vivid. When he talks about those distant days, the memories come alive; they are echoes of a way of life that has all but disappeared from the American scene.

Our farm was seventeen miles from Bayfield, the nearest town with a high school. Unfortunately there was no school bus—and therefore no way for me to get to school; so my parents decided that I should attend Lincoln High School in Park Falls where I could stay with my sister Eleanor and her husband, Oscar.

Eleanor lived quite a distance from the high school; so she packed a lunch for me every day. Another sister, Mildred, lived about half way between Eleanor's house and the school. I'd drop my bag lunch off at Mildred's on my way to school and walk there during the noon hour to have lunch with her and my nieces and nephews.

I loved those days at Lincoln High. I made some wonderful friends, and I was active in the chorus. Every year we staged an operetta, and I was always lucky enough to get a solo part. When I think back on my vocal talents, I have to wonder how bad the other kids were if the director chose me for a leading role!

I used to love getting ready for the operetta, because the whole cast stayed for hours after school; and then we'd gather at the local hamburger parlor for supper—a burger and a malt or a bottle of "pop."

My parents sent me a dollar a month for spending money, and I thought I was the world's luckiest boy. Movies only cost a dime; so I learned to manage my money and stretch that dollar as far as it would go. I added a little to my bankroll by helping neighbors saw and pile wood for the winter.

If my cash was running low, Eleanor or Mildred would give me a sandwich for an evening snack. I don't think I ever got back to Eleanor's when there wasn't something hot waiting for me—a plate of food in the warming oven of her wood cook stove, or a pot of soup or chili simmering on top. Eleanor was an excellent cook, and it never mattered how many people were around; there was always enough food for everybody, and Eleanor loved dishing it up.

The first snowfall was a tremendously exciting event, because then I could begin skiing to school. If there was a play practice or choral rehearsal, I stayed after school until dark. I was never frightened while I skied back to Eleanor's; there was something very calming about the hush of the countryside in the dark.

I went home for the holidays on the Greyhound bus. My parents sent me the fare, along with instructions to buy a round-trip ticket so I'd save a few cents. The Greyhound left Park Falls early in the morning and went to Ashland, where I had to transfer to a small bus line that traveled between Ashland and Bayfield. The trip from Park Falls to Bayfield was about four hours, and usually I arrived in Bayfield by 11:30 in the morning. Dad and one of my brothers would pick me up at the Bayfield Hotel, where the bus stopped, and we would drive the seventeen miles home.

On Thanksgiving morning in 1939, I boarded the bus in Park Falls. Snow had begun to fall, and it kept falling all the way to Ashland. Because of the slippery roads, the bus was late, and I missed the first connecting bus from Ashland to Bayfield. We didn't have a telephone at home, and even if we had, I don't think I would have known how to make a long distance call—especially one that would have been collect, since I was almost out of money.

I decided to catch the next bus to Bayfield, scheduled to leave around noon. After I got off at Bayfield and stood around waiting for a half hour, I began to feel somewhat anxious when I realized that no one was there to pick me up for the ride home.

The snow had stopped, but it was turning bitter cold. I decided to hitchhike home; I was sure that someone would come along and give me a lift. By

this time it was nearly one o'clock in the afternoon; I had no overshoes on, but I set out bravely carrying my suitcase.

By the time I had walked out of Bayfield and onto Highway 13, I began to notice that there were no car tracks in the snow—not even a snowplow had gone through! I had a sinking feeling when I realized my predicament: it was Thanksgiving afternoon, and anyone who was driving would either have left early in the morning or gone back home because of the storm.

I still believed that I'd be lucky, and that someone would come along, or that my Dad and brother were late because of the snowy roads, and they would surely come driving up. I kept walking against the wind, my feet beginning to freeze; I ran, on and off, just to warm up.

The suitcase seemed to get heavier with every mile, and at times I thought of hiding it alongside the road and coming back for it later, but I worried that I might lose my clothing. So I lugged it as I walked all of those seventeen miles, getting colder and more exhausted by the hour. Not one car ever came from either direction!

Our house was about a quarter mile off of Highway 13 and sat on a hill overlooking Lake Superior. When I got to that road, I knew I was home—I had made it! It was almost dark, but that last little stretch seemed to go very fast.

When I walked in the house my family was shocked, and Mother began to cry. They had driven to Bayfield to pick me up, but since I wasn't on the bus they assumed I had decided not to come home because of the storm. They had finished their Thanksgiving dinner, but another plate was lovingly prepared for me. The turkey, stuffing, mashed potatoes, gravy and all the rest of the trimmings tasted like heaven to a weary and very cold sixteen-year-old boy.

Dad had had the battery charged so that we could listen to the radio that night, and I'm sure there were several games of cribbage before I went up to my room and crawled into bed, warm and safe at last.

Mother told me the next day that she thought my brother should have gone back to Bayfield a second time. She figured I missed the bus, or that the bus was late.

Mothers are always right. They were then, too.

Bea Bourgeois

Carnival

The forest is a pageant of beauty
As autumn steals away;
Yet a thread of sadness is woven
Through the lavish Romany days.
The trees that were green all summer
Have donned their carnival dress,
And each seems to vie with the other
To look lovelier than the rest.
The maples are gay, carefree gypsies
In tatters of yellow and red;
Even the proud oaks are rakish
With crimson wreaths on their heads;
The ashes are regal in purple,
While birches flash bangles of gold,
And the viburnums' magenta pales
By the scarlet dogwood so bold;
The tiniest bush has been glorified
In draperies of russet or wine,
And the slenderest little sapling
Is gowned like a fair Columbine.
The festival soon will be ended
When the north wind starts to blow,
Taking the costumes with it
To be changed into white shrouds of snow.

                    Milly Walton

Other seeds fell on good soil and brought forth grain, some a hundredfold, some sixty, some thirty.

Matthew 13:8 (RSV)

November Seeds

Diane Skinner

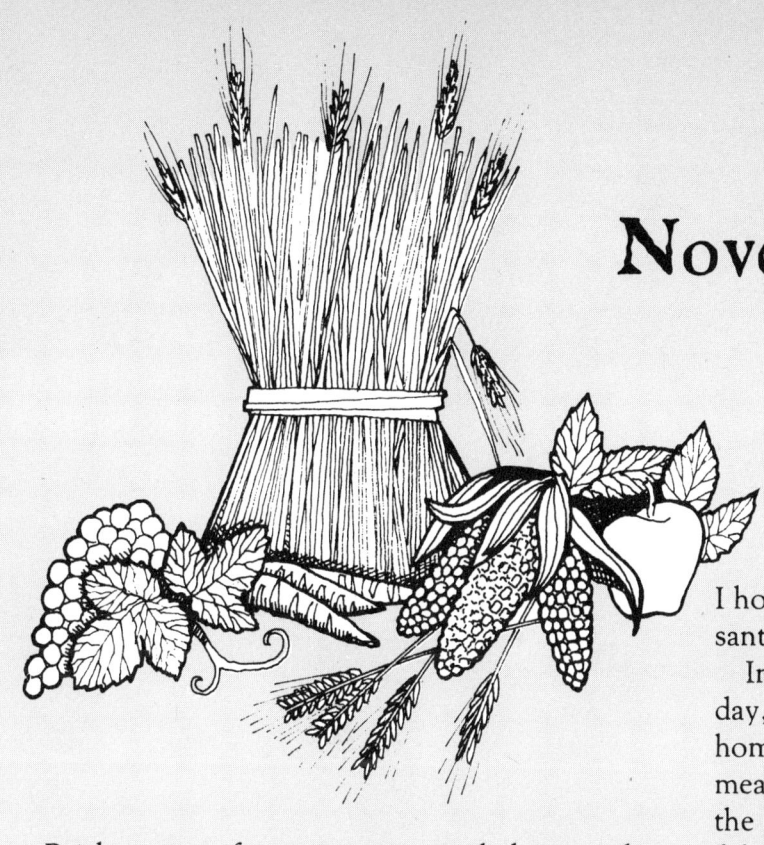

Brisk gusts of autumn air rippled my nylon parka as I threaded my way across a smoky gray mountain. Hiking alone, I felt refreshed by the quietness of the barren Blue Ridge. Taking our small son on his first hunting trip, my husband, Mike, had left me behind. Grateful for a few moments alone, I walked on in solitude—communing with nature.

Stopping to rest at a lofty overlook, I gazed at the towering mountains, overwhelmed by their vastness. Surely my awe, this sense of exhilarating wonder, must have been the sentiment of earlier pioneers, the Scotch and Irish stock who settled here long ago.

Reflections on this sturdy band of pilgrims, who homesteaded high on the Blue Ridge Mountains, ignited thoughts of this month's celebration. Somehow Thanksgiving would be different this year, I thought through misting eyes. Being eight hundred miles from our "homeland," we had broken traditional family ties and, instead, planned to bring in the season with newfound friends. Employing the customs of earlier forefathers, I had secured an empty cabin deep in the forest and readied it with corn shocks and pumpkins. Five picnic tables covered with white paper would adequately seat our guests, I had estimated, while holding the odd assortment of seasonal food: venison, turkey, Virginia ham, baked beans, squash, wild rice, dressing, fresh buttered rolls, succotash, homemade apple butter, pumpkin pie and plum pudding. Wistfully I hoped Mike and Jamie would bring back a pheasant to add to the menu.

Inspired with my thoughts of the coming holiday, I arose from my rock and started the trek homeward. To the east, vast stretches of open meadow now were a musty green, hibernating for the oncoming winter. Looking over the autumn foliage, I reminisced of earlier flowers, exotics and grasses which had previously graced the hillside. Thoughts of the variety of plants produced by European grain bags passed through my mind. Through stowaway and explorer, the seeds had come, making their way over a salty Atlantic and lodging on American soil.

Spurred on by rumbling pains of hunger, I took one last wistful gaze at the open meadow. Yes, like the seeds of vegetation, Mike and I had also been transported miles from our homeland and had attached ourselves to this big rugged mountain. Putting down my roots of a home and a family, I reminisced of previous roots driven deep in the ground by earlier settlers. Thoughtfully I pondered my own existence and contributions I was presently sprinkling on my soil. Hadn't I brought with me my mother's faith? Why couldn't I transplant her Christianity in this mountain by sowing seeds of faith, seeds of hope, and seeds of love? With God's help some should take root and grow—I knew it, and like the flowers of the meadow, they would multiply and produce again. Flourishing they would color dull lives with God's beauty and brighten the most humble surrounding.

As I reached my empty cabin and opened the door, I was happy and thankful. Not only could I praise God for a bountiful time of harvest, but also for my mother's faith which I had reaped and was now able to transport miles away and scatter as seeds on barren soil.

O Give Thanks

Harold W. Rock

In this country we should find it easy to be thankful because of the many blessings that are ours. We spend millions of dollars to reduce our waistlines due to overeating and drinking, whereas most people in the world struggle from dawn to dusk to gain a full meal. We have come to expect a house, or at least a suite of rooms, as our living quarters, whereas most people of the world are happy to have a single room of their own. When we describe our way of life to people in other countries, they frequently think we are exaggerating our standard of living and that we are really talking about only the wealthy. Visitors from Asia, Africa and South America, while startled by our material wealth, are even more amazed by the complete freedom we have in publicly expressing our opinions, in worshipping, in obtaining an education, and in selecting employment.

Besides the freedoms and opportunities that we enjoy, there are many natural blessings inherent in this country. Our land is rich in natural resources including many minerals, a great variety of useful plants and animals, a great supply of fresh water and large areas of tillable soil. We have literally become the "bread basket of the world" as we continue to produce great quantities of wheat, corn, soybeans, and other farm crops. Our people not only have a plentiful food supply, but they have a great variety of tasty and wholesome food products. As a result, our children have become increasingly bigger, healthier and more active.

Covering many parts of our country are forests that consist of a great variety of attractive and useful trees. In the United States there are over eight hundred tree species from which we obtain building materials, paper, fuel, resins, food products and many other side products. The shrubs and herbs that cover the forest floor are exceedingly valuable as a source of food and, more importantly, as a cover and shelter for the soil and the developing plants and animals.

Often the least appreciated of our blessings are the wild flowers and grasses that cover and beautify our fields, swamps and woodlands. Usually these herbs are referred to as "weeds" and too often are ignored and destroyed. Communities actually spend taxpayers' money to mow them down, when in reality they are not only harmless but extremely beneficial in covering our countryside. Our native grasses and flowering herbs are hardy, beautiful and non-allergenic, contrary to public opinion. Only the ragweeds normally are allergenic, and these plants will grow only in disturbed areas. Such native flowers as pasque flower, shooting star, purple coneflower, blazing star, yellow ladyslipper, cardinal flower and many more are used directly in our formal and informal gardens with no modifications. Instead of overlooking the beauty and value of our native plants, we could allow them to grow alongside our highways to good advantage. Since most of these prairie plants thrive in the hot, dry summer weather, we could have beautiful, blooming roadsides and park areas at that time of year. There would be no need for cutting, and consequently there would be no layer of brown, mowed grass.

In nature we are also blessed with a great variety of plant communities because of a great variation in rainfall and geological features. Unfortunately, unique areas, such as wetlands, deserts, rocky slopes and sand dunes, are often considered waste areas; in reality they are fascinating complex gardens of specialized flora and fauna. Hopefully, these unique plant and animal systems will survive.

Only a few of our blessings have been mentioned. Americans are often unaware of the rich and diverse natural heritage we have. Because of the great wealth with which our country has been endowed, we are reminded of the words of King David, O give thanks unto the Lord,

For He is good,

For His mercy endureth forever.

December 7, 1941: A Date Long Remembered

At 2:30 P.M. (EST) on December 7, 1941, six million families across the nation were listening to calm Sunday afternoon radio programs such as the New York Philharmonic Symphony concert. Suddenly, all networks broke in with the shocking bulletin: "The Japanese have attacked Pearl Harbor by air. President Roosevelt has just announced . . . ." The sharp words cut into the tranquillity of that Sunday afternoon and carved the word WAR into the American way of life.

Only a few hours earlier, shortly after 6:30 A.M. by Hawaiian clocks, an unidentified midget submarine was sighted and destroyed in the restricted waters close to the entrance of Pearl Harbor. The first wave of Japanese bombers had already taken off from Admiral Nagumo's aircraft carriers over two hundred miles north in the Pacific Ocean and were flying above a layer of clouds toward the Hawaiian Islands. The radar watch on Oahu had officially closed down at 7 A.M., but two operators had stayed a few more minutes and reported that they had detected a large number of aircraft at a range of 132 miles. The inexperienced officer who received their report did not believe it and assumed they had simply detected a dozen American bombers expected on a delivery flight to the island. So without opposition, forty Japanese torpedo bombers, fifty high-level bombers, fifty dive bombers, and an escort of fifty fighters reached Oahu a little before 8 A.M. and attacked.

The stillness of the peaceful Sunday morning was broken by the piercing whine of dive bombers and sharp chatter of machine guns. The attack on the airfields had barely started before the first bombs and torpedoes hit the sitting targets moored at Ford Island in Pearl Harbor. Over one hundred more bombers followed in a second wave. In an hour and a half the Japanese destroyed four battleships, crippled two, sank half a dozen cruisers and destroyers, destroyed or damaged over two hundred aircraft, and killed almost three thousand soldiers, sailors, airmen, and civilians, while leaving over one thousand wounded. The Japanese lost only fifty-five men and twenty-nine planes.

Many Americans lost their lives before they were aware of the attack. Others fought courageously, manning antiaircraft guns even after receiving orders to abandon ship. The rage to strike back was so strong that men even fired pistols as the enemy planes swooped low. Similar rage was felt later on the mainland. U.S. citizens who had been reluctant to initiate any direct involvement in the war were now eager to fight. This was the turning point when American spectators became active participants in a worldwide confrontation.

U.S. citizens had been so strongly opposed to war that they had to be aroused by a catastrophic event before they would abandon the illusion that they could isolate themselves from the rest of the world. The country changed overnight. Civilian pursuits became unimportant; only the war seemed to matter. The United States had already been sending war materials to countries resisting the advance of Japan, Germany, and Italy, realizing that helping Allies in any part of the world strengthened the U.S. defense. And now America was ready to fight alongside Great Britain, France, and other Allies in order to preserve democracy and maintain individual freedom. Americans were anxious to enlist and help in any way they could. As it was, the attack created such unanimous support for Franklin D. Roosevelt's declaration of war on Japan that some people, such as Admiral Kimmel who commanded the fleet at Pearl Harbor, alleged that the President knew about the plan before the attack and let it happen to force America's hand.

The Japanese ambassador to the United States had been conducting peace negotiations in Washington, D.C. when Japan took advantage of that strategic opportunity to attack without warning. The Japanese government had deliberately deceived the U.S. and for good reason. Germany had promised Japan it would share in the spoils after the war and receive complete control of the Far East and Pacific, but only if it would attack the U.S. Within the span of twenty-four hours, Japan launched a surprise offensive extending throughout the Pacific area, attacking not only Hawaii, but Malaya, Hong Kong, Guam, Wake Island, Midway Island, and the Philippine Islands.

The aim had been to put the U.S. Pacific Fleet out of action and cut supply lines to allied nations. However, the Pacific Fleet suffered only a temporary setback. Two U.S. aircraft carriers had been sent out of Pearl Harbor on missions and fortunately escaped destruction. Many of the damaged ships were repaired and returned to action. The U.S. naval base was left intact, suffering little damage to workshops, docks, and other installations, allowing it to remain a repair and refitting station and the control center for air and naval operations in the Pacific.

On December 8, sixty million Americans heard Roosevelt's historic broadcast about the "dastardly attack." He called it a "date which will live in infamy." His prediction held true, and the lives lost in the tragedy have not been forgotten. Every year, thousands of tourists stop in Oahu to see the memorial at Pearl Harbor, the most visited spot in the Hawaiian Islands. Visitors cruise the harbor, passing the famed Battleship Row, on their way to pay tribute to the 1,102 men still entombed in the sunken U.S.S. *Arizona*. The impressive Arizona Memorial, a bridge of white concrete spanning the hull of the submerged battleship, stands as a reminder of treachery that can endanger American freedom.

This year marks the Fortieth Anniversary of the bombing of Pearl Harbor. After the disaster, Roosevelt promised that the American people would "win through to absolute victory." And so they did. The peace that had been shattered took several years to regain. In this time of Thanksgiving, Americans can be thankful that freedom was preserved and peace was recreated out of the ashes of Pearl Harbor.

Gale Wiersum Clapper

November

November is all mist and mystery,
A month of undertones and muted grays,
When secret dreams become reality
And wonder walks down curving woodland ways.
It is a pause before the shawl of snow
Has silenced insects, turned the nights as still
As idle moments summer lovers know,
Who drowse in clover on a sun-warmed hill.
The hurrying is over and the year
Slopes gently down to comfortable sleep.
Indoors the fire of applewood flames clear,
As days close in and nights grow dark and deep.
Softly in this mist-shrouded interval
We hear time play the year's recessional.

                      Alice Mackenzie Swaim

Harvest Home

Henry Alford

Come, ye thankful people, come,
Raise the song of harvest home:
All is safely gathered in,
Ere the winter storms begin;
God, our Maker, doth provide
For our wants to be supplied.
Come to God's own temple, come,
Raise the song of harvest home.

All the world is God's own field,
Fruit unto His praise to yield;
Wheat and tares together sown,
Unto joy or sorrow grown;
First the blade, and then the ear,
Then the full corn shall appear.
Lord of harvest, grant that we
Wholesome grain and pure may be.

For the Lord our God shall come
And shall take His harvest home;
From His field shall in that day
All offenses purge away;
Give His angels charge at last,
In the fire the tares to cast;
But the fruitful ears to store
In His garner evermore.

Even so, Lord, quickly come
To Thy final harvest home;
Gather Thou Thy people in,
Free from sorrow, free from sin;
There, forever purified,
In Thy presence to abide.
Come, with all Thine angels, come,
Raise the glorious harvest home.

With Each Thanksgiving Dinner
Craig E. Sathoff

With each Thanksgiving dinner,
There's a thought of yesterday
And Indians helping Pilgrims
Get the feasting underway.

There're squash and wild turkey,
And there's fresh-baked pumpkin, too,
And succotash from corn and beans,
And berries sweetly stewed.

With each Thanksgiving dinner,
There's a time to bow and pray,
To thank the Lord for our America,
Both now and yesterday.

To thank the Lord for family unity
And loved ones gathered near
Who share in the festivities
Of grand Thanksgiving cheer.

With each Thanksgiving dinner
There's much to thank Him for,
And every year that passes by
Brings many blessings more.

Thanksgiving Grace
Louise Darcy

O Lord, we know that all things come from Thee,
And as we bow our heads upon this day,
Thanking Thee for another harvest yield,
Our gratitude is boundless as we pray.

Lord of all life, we know Thy mighty hand
Encircles everyone throughout the year.
With deep devotion now we offer up
The thankful homage of those gathered here.

The Crowning Touch

The traditional Thanksgiving dinner—yes, we've waited an entire year to partake of this succulent feast. And though we feel quite content after one or even several generous helpings of turkey and complementary trimmings, the eating is not over yet—not without a sliver of delicious homemade pie. No treat can compare with a freshly baked pie prepared when the fruits of the harvest season are at their peak. Golden pumpkin spiced just right or rich, savory mincemeat—now, which will it be?

> Mince and pumpkin pies in sight,
> Each a holiday delight.
> Haven't made my mind up, quite—
> Yes, I'm sure my choice will be,
> Kindly, some of both for me!

Tender Piecrust

Makes 1 9-inch crust.

- ½ cup whole wheat flour
- ½ cup oat flour, or oatmeal finely ground in a blender
- ½ teaspoon salt
- ¼ cup butter or margarine
- 2 tablespoons cold water

Mix flours and salt. Cut in butter with a pastry cutter until crumbly. Add cold water, sprinkling a few drops at a time over the top and mixing lightly with a fork. Press dough into a ball; roll between sheets of wax paper or press into the pie pan. If baking crust before filling, prick with a fork. Bake at 450° for 10 to 12 minutes, or until lightly browned. Double the recipe for a two-crust pie.

Pumpkin Pecan Pie

Makes 1 9-inch pie.

- 1 unbaked Tender Piecrust
- 3 tablespoons butter or margarine
- ⅓ cup firmly packed brown sugar
- ⅓ cup chopped pecans

Cream butter with brown sugar; add pecans. Spread over unbaked crust. Bake at 450° for 10 minutes, remove from oven, and reduce heat to 350°.

Pumpkin Filling

- 1½ cups cooked or canned pumpkin
- 1 teaspoon vanilla extract
- 3 eggs
- 1 cup firmly packed brown sugar
- 1½ teaspoons pumpkin pie spice
- ½ teaspoon salt
- 1 cup evaporated milk
- ½ cup water

Mix pumpkin, vanilla, eggs, brown sugar, spice and salt. Scald evaporated milk and water. Combine pumpkin mixture with scalded milk. Pour into baked crust. Bake at 350° for 50 minutes, or until center is almost set. Do not overbake; custard will set as it cools. Cool completely.

Crumbly Crust Mincemeat Pie

Makes 1 9-inch pie.

- Double recipe of Tender Piecrust
- ⅓ cup firmly packed brown sugar
- 1 teaspoon ground cinnamon
- 1 egg white

Follow directions for piecrust; before adding the water, divide in half. Add brown sugar and cinnamon to half the piecrust; mix until crumbly; set aside. Add only 2 tablespoons cold water to the other half and prepare as directed in the recipe. Fit into a 9-inch pie pan. Brush with egg white and place in a preheated 425° oven for 3 minutes. Fill with the prepared Mincemeat. Sprinkle with crumbly cinnamon crust mixture. Bake for 25 to 30 minutes, or until crust is browned. Cool.

Mincemeat

- 4 cups pared, chopped tart apples
- 2 tablespoons butter
- ⅔ cup seedless raisins
- ½ cup honey
- 1 tablespoon citron
- ½ teaspoon ground cinnamon
- ¼ teaspoon ground cloves
- ¼ teaspoon salt

Place all ingredients in a saucepan. Heat to boiling on medium heat, stirring occasionally. When mixture boils, turn to low heat and simmer, covered, for 10 minutes. Uncover and continue cooking until most of the juice evaporates.

Autumn's Magic Brush

He is a lavish painter
Who gilds an autumn tree.
He dips his brush in liquid gold
That flows unsparingly.

He is a daring painter
Upon whose palette spreads
Crimson, scarlet, burgundy, mauve—
The galaxy of reds.

He is a thoughtful painter
Who leaves some trees still green,
Restraining his autumnal brush
For lingering notes of spring.

He is a master artist
Whose landscapes blaze before us,
And we are inarticulate
Beholding autumn's forest.

                Marie Hunter Dawson

We Pause

Serenely golden are the hills and fields.
The fruits are gathered, and the grains are stored.
Now autumn sunlight on the tranquil earth
Is like a benediction of the Lord.

The rush of planting and the harvest done,
We pause to look across the peaceful land
With gratitude for all the blessings poured
In rich abundance from God's gracious hand.

                Gail Brook Burket

Fall

Catherine Jasper

The music of fall is wild and free.
It beats with a pulsing ecstasy
Through the dark of night
  when wild geese cry
And beat their wings
  through a sullen sky,

When trees their burden
  of bright leaves spill
A golden treasure upon the hill,
And nature chants in exultation
Of God's great gifts to all creation.

Autumn Morning
Louise Darcy

Hold this gay morning
Close to the heart;
Hear wild geese calling
As southward they start.

Now trees are flaming;
Red conquers green;
Orange and yellow
Brighten each scene.

Hold this clear morning
Close to the heart;
Thank God who made it
With hallowed art.

This Time of Year
Grace E. Easley

There's a touch of sweet nostalgia
About this time of year,
A whimsical illusiveness
That borders on the rare;
Each multicolored moment
Reflected through the screen
Of inner thoughts that brush the realm
Of sensed and yet unseen!

Crocheted across the countryside
In intricate design,
An afghan made of silver frost
By Hands that are divine,
And through the woodland's manor,
Dispelling shadowed gloom,
Golden threads of sunlight
From the Master's busy loom!

Through the symphony of silence,
The wild geese overhead
And in their throats a lyric
Such as man has never read;
And my humble heart is thankful
For this special time of year,
For no sermon any greater
Than these feathered wings I hear!

The Hush of Snow

A glistening world awaits the day—
The hush of snow is everywhere;
Even the wind, with cautious breath,
Is still as a whispered prayer.

All the trees are draped with lace
Spun of gossamer from a cloud;
Myriad bits of snowflakes white
Wove of themselves this shroud

To cover the barren earth and roots,
Dreaming of warmth and returning spring.
But now, responsive hearts concede
Snow is truly a beautiful thing!

Rowena Cheney

ACKNOWLEDGMENTS

AFTER HARVESTINGS; COUNTRYMAN'S THANKSGIVING; FREEDOM FROM WANT; A POEM FOR THANKSGIVING by Edith Shaw Butler. All from AMERICAN AGRICULTURIST, used with permission. THIS TIME OF YEAR by Grace E. Easley. From FINDING BEAUTY by Grace E. Easley, Copyright © 1974 by Grace E. Easley. HOMAGE TO NOVEMBER by Elizabeth Searle Lamb. From TODAY AND EVERY DAY by Elizabeth Searle Lamb, Copyright © 1970 by Unity School of Christianity. A THANKSGIVING MEDITATION (originally titled: A THANKSGIVING PRAYER) by Bernice Maddux. Previously published in POSITIVE LIVING, November 1978. Reprinted with permission of the author. RIVER BEND by Jessie Wilmore Murton. From her book GRACE NOTES, Copyright © 1960 by Review and Herald Publishing Association. Reprinted with permission. MY ABC'S OF FRUITS AND VEGETABLES by Caroline M. Nye. Previously published in FARM WIFE NEWS, P. O. Box 643, Milwaukee, WI 53201. Used with permission of the author. A LEGACY OF LAUGHTER by Colleen L. Reece. Reprinted with permission of SEPTEMBER DAYS Magazine. Our sincere thanks to the following author whose address we were unable to locate: Linda Lowe for AUTUMN.

COLOR ART AND PHOTO CREDITS
(in order of appearance)

Front and back covers, Gerald Koser; inside front and back covers, NOVEMBER STILLNESS, R. Lardinois; Thanksgiving reverence, Fred Sieb; Chrysanthemums, Fred Sieb; Red house near Island Pond, Vermont, Alpha Photo Associates; Harvest display, Fred Sieb; Fruit-filled wheelbarrow, Alpha Photo Associates; Young companions, George A. Robinson; Houses along Rescue Lake, Vermont, Fred Sieb; Peaceful stream, Alpha Photo Associates; Swans, H. Armstrong Roberts; Candlelight thanks, Colour Library International (USA) Limited; Pantry corner, Colour Library International (USA) Limited; PILGRIM FAMILY, John Walter; Rustic tabletop, Fred Sieb; AUTUMN WALK, Ernest Smith; White-tailed buck, Three Lions, Inc.; Milkweed seed pod, Bob Taylor; Forest floor near Kearsarge, New Hampshire, Fred Sieb; Fringed gentian, Gerald Koser; Sierra Nevada farm near Bishop, California, Ed Cooper; THANKSGIVING IN NEW ENGLAND, Missouri Jenkins, Three Lions, Inc.; Thanksgiving feast, H. Armstrong Roberts; Harvest scenic near North Conway, New Hampshire, Fred Sieb; Farmstead near Granby, Colorado, Ed Cooper; Picturesque church, Fred Sieb; Light snow in Yosemite Valley, California, Ed Cooper.

'Tis the season . . .

. . . for holiday good wishes! What better way to express your heartfelt sentiments to friends and relatives than with gift subscriptions to Ideals?

Our next issue, Christmas Ideals, has been a part of family holiday celebrations for almost forty years. The special moments and traditions families and friends share are portrayed in glowing color photography and artwork along with touching prose and poetry. Enjoy the magic and warmth of Christmas in: a collection of favorite Christmas carols; the poem "Santa's List" accompanied by a Norman Rockwell painting; an article featuring delicious Christmas recipes from France, Germany, and Poland; and the poem "Bethlehem's Town" which recounts the Nativity story. The new 1981 Christmas Ideals is sure to make everyone's holiday brighter, whether they're six or sixty!

Choose either a one-year or two-year subscription to convey your good wishes to the special people in your life. And, subscribe for yourself . . . enjoy the beauty of Ideals all year long!